THE Go-To Church

Post MegaChurch Growth

Bryan Collier

Abingdon Press
Nashville

THE GO-TO CHURCH

POST MEGACHURCH GROWTH

Copyright © 2013 by Abingdon Press

This book is printed on acid-free paper.

Library of Congress Cataloging-in-Publication Data

Collier, Bryan D.
  The go-to church : post megachurch growth / Bryan D. Collier.
    pages cm
  ISBN 978-1-4267-5325-1 (pbk. : alk. paper) 1. Multi-site churches.
2. Church growth. I. Title.
  BV637.95.C65 2013
  254'.5—dc23

                                                              2013001885

Scripture quotations are taken from the *Holy Bible,* New Living Translation, copyright © 1996. Used by permission of Tyndale House Publishers, Inc., Wheaton, Illinois 60189. All rights reserved.

13 14 15 16 17 18 19 20 21 22—10 9 8 7 6 5 4 3 2 1

MANUFACTURED IN THE UNITED STATES OF AMERICA

To my family,
Wendy, Olivia, and Houston,
and The Orchard Family:
Thanks for loving Jesus and loving
others enough to try new things!

CONTENTS

Being a Go-To Church

Introduction

Do you have a dream of vibrancy for your local church? Do you desire to be fruitful for Christ's kingdom? Do you desire to reach the unchurched and unreached in your community? Do you feel at a loss for new ideas to attract people to your church? If so, then become a **Go-To Church**. Become a church that decides to go-to rather than wait for the world to come-to; ask a different set of questions; live by a different set of rules; change the way you think and live and serve and you can see your desires and God's dreams realized.

In the summer of 1998, God sent my wife, Wendy, and me to Tupelo, Mississippi, to begin a new United Methodist faith community. Tupelo was a fast-growing furniture town near the community where I grew up.

The prospect of starting a new church was both daunting and exciting, and we moved to town with passion, vision, and a dream.

During the year prior to our arrival in Tupelo, we had been part of a Doctor of Ministry residential program that focused on Biblical Preaching and Leadership. We had accepted that residential fellowship with a specific group of people in mind—those who did not go to church for any reason. My wife and I both grew up in church; in church vernacular, we were both "lifers." But we both knew many people in the Tupelo region who had been burned by church, did not understand church, did not like church, or could not see faith's relevance to their everyday lives. With these people in mind, we moved to Tupelo and went to work.

When we began to consider a strategy for reaching that group of people and being the kind of church they would consider attending, it became obvious that there was a group of people who had faced the same challenge, had the same heart, and had been largely successful at it—the first disciples. The fact that every person in all of history, past, present, or future, who had ever believed in the resurrection and trusted Jesus with their lives could trace the beginning of hearing the good news back to one of those original twelve was a strong testimony that they had a great plan and tremendous resources to get the job done. With that in mind, we began to search the Scriptures closely for insights that might inform and empower the work God had given us to do in the Tupelo region.

When the early church began, there were a few more people involved than just the original twelve. However, it is clear from Scripture that Jesus firmly placed the responsibility of interesting the disinterested on them. We too felt that same responsibility, and with that responsibility came an overwhelming feeling that we were in over our heads. But Scripture also comforted us as we recognized that God's story is full of accounts of God giving human beings monumental tasks. However, it is also God's practice to give the resources and the direction necessary to get the job done.

God told Abraham that he would be the father of a multitude when Abraham had no children. When Abraham believed, God gave Abraham a son and descendants as numerous as the stars. God told Noah to build an ark to save his family and two of every species on the earth at the time because an enormous flood would come to destroy every living thing. Noah, with God's blueprint, built the ark, and God brought the animals to Noah so he could put them on the boat. David faced Goliath, Elijah challenged the four hundred prophets of Baal, and Moses faced down Egypt's greatest Pharaoh—and these are just a few of the stories of God giving human beings monumental tasks and the resources to do them.

We should not be surprised that Jesus gave the disciples the monumental task of reaching the world. Jesus was not giving the disciples some motivational take-the-world-by-storm kind of speech. It was Jesus' intention that those disciples would perpetuate the task he had begun in such a way that it might one day come to completion.

Wendy and I wanted to be faithful in that work and to be part of a community of faith that wanted to be faithful in that work, and so we began to plan, dream, and cast vision for a community of faith called The Orchard, which would be an orchard not only in name but also in practice.

The Orchard and an Orchard

This name and this dream were birthed as we became entrenched in John 15.

John 15 is divided into two large sections around a pivotal verse, John 15:16. Jesus announces, "You didn't choose me. I chose you. I appointed you to go and produce lasting fruit, so that the Father will give you whatever you ask for, using my name." Jesus uses multiple images for what he wants disciples to be doing, but here he clearly points out that he expects us to "bear fruit."

In teaching and leading, we wanted to be clear not only about what Jesus wanted us to do but also how he wanted us to do it. There are, depending on which version you read, approximately forty-three mentions of the word *fruit* in the New Testament. If you begin to group those forty-three occurrences, then you find that they begin to arrange themselves into three distinct groups. I titled these groups and identified a representative Scripture reference for each group as a way of trying to understand what Jesus meant by "fruit" so we can determine just how we are to produce it.

The first fruit group might be called *Presentation.* Jesus says, "Yes, just as you can identify a tree by its fruit, so you can identify people by their actions" (Matthew 7:20). Jesus is indicating that you can tell where someone is rooted by the kind of fruit on the end of the branch. If he or she is rooted in Christ, then that person will produce a very different kind of fruit than if he or she is rooted in the self or in anything other than Christ.

The second fruit group might be called *Progress.* In John 17:17 Jesus prays that God the Father would make his disciples holy by setting them apart in truth. This holy-making that Jesus prays for is a little more clearly understood when we read a passage from Paul's letter to the Galatians. Paul writes, "But the Holy Spirit produces this kind of fruit in our lives: love, joy, peace, patience, kindness, goodness, faithfulness, gentleness, and self-control" (Galatians 5:22-23). The Holy Spirit is at work progressively making us more fully into the likeness of Christ. The Spirit is producing fruit in our lives.

The third representative group is called *People*. Jesus clearly says, "the fruit [that the harvesters] harvest is people brought to eternal life" (John 4:36).

Jesus calls the disciples to fruit-bearing, and a careful examination of the New Testament points to this fruit as helping people become more rooted in Christ so they can grow up to be like Christ and can introduce people to Christ. This is what Jesus means by fruit-bearing.

How?

After some clarification of what we were supposed to be doing, we turned to the question of how we go about this work. In the first section of John 15 (verses 1-15) Jesus reminds the disciples that he is the Vine and they are the branches and apart from him they can do nothing. It is clear that he does not mean some things— he means no-thing. Withered and fruitless because of disconnection, the branches will be gathered and discarded in the fire. So the first message to the disciples is a reminder to maintain an ongoing vibrant connection to the Source of wisdom, strength, clarity, and power that will make their fruit-bearing mission possible. Because we were trying to connect disconnected people, we wanted to make this image as clear as possible, so we called this staying connected emphasis "growing deep." An orchard is a place that is devoted to the cultivation of fruit for Christ's kingdom by helping people grow deep in the love of Jesus.

The second section of John 15 (verses 18-27) lets the disciples know just how difficult their task is going to be. It seems that in this section Jesus overuses the word *hate*, but Jesus knows the reception that the disciples are going to get will mirror the one that he receives. Yet, he wants them to know that he will send "the Advocate— the Spirit of truth" (John 15:26) and that in the power of that Spirit they are to testify about him as those who knew him best. For clarity's sake, we called this outreach emphasis "branching out." An orchard is a place that is devoted to the cultivation of fruit for Christ's kingdom by helping people grow deep in the love of Jesus and branching out to others with that love.

The clarity of that vision and mission has guided our dreams and hopes from the very first day until now. We earnestly desired to plant a community of faith so in tune with God's call and passion that it would be pliable enough to reshape itself continually in order to remain a useful instrument to accomplish God's purposes. It would have a God-centered intuitiveness about how to communicate the eternal truth of the good news to an ever-changing culture. This community of faith would not be encumbered by the politics of power, and personal opinion would not be the deciding factor in matters of governance. This community of faith would clearly speak the message of faith in the language of the people, and it would hold every tradition, practice, and movement lightly while holding to the unchanging gospel firmly. This would be a community of faith who had a clear understanding of what God was calling them to do and how God was calling them uniquely to do it. Moreover, this would be a people whose structure was streamlined enough to actually be this kind of community and not merely talk or dream about it.

The Orchard set its sights on becoming *an orchard*. This fruitfulness through growing deep and branching out has been our aim as we have pursued this vision for the last thirteen years. With the twenty-thousand unreached people in our region on our hearts and minds, we have had to be an adaptable organism that responds to the needs of the people we are trying to reach without abandoning who God has called us to be as God's representatives in this community. This need for adaptability not only opened our eyes to our need to be constantly changing in order to meet people where they are, but it also opened our eyes to new communities and new ideas of how this adaptable spirit could help us reach them. This continual challenge to change in order to be effective poses great risks and presents great opportunities.

Because we are constantly changing, people who fell in love with a particular practice of ministry at The Orchard risk falling out of love with us when we no longer practice that ministry or method that they loved. But the greater risk is to take no risk at all—determining what we do and doing it for decades even though it no longer effectively produces what we were called to produce: disciples. It is the opportunity to try new things to reach new people that must drive the church who would be fruitful for Christ's kingdom.

Our dream is that we would be an orchard, not just a church called The Orchard. An orchard produces fruit. It doesn't fall in love with the idea of being an orchard. It exists to bear fruit. Planting, pruning, and uprooting are all parts of being fruitful—of realizing a vision to reach the unreached in our region, to help them grow to be like Jesus, and to send them out to act like Jesus in order that they may introduce people to Jesus.

Countercultural?

Taking risks for the advancement of the gospel should not be countercultural in the Church, but it seems too often that it is. The mainline church has been in decline for four decades while churches that are nimble enough to respond to cultural changes and focused enough to remember why they exist thrive.

Large organizations like my denomination (The United Methodist Church) have neither the capacity nor the desire to change. By sheer size, they have garnered a following and resources that let them sustain their existence long after their effectiveness has gone. With layers of approval and resources spread so thinly over hundreds if not thousands of emphases, these denominations make decisions and implement policy that are aimed at survival, not effective accomplishment of Christ's mission.

These denominations can serve as a macrocosm of local churches that are no better off. Because they exist without the end "product" clearly in mind, there is no way to honestly examine whether or not they are effective. With no clear scorecard, many mainline churches (just like their mainline denominational parent) do what they have always done even though effectiveness is long gone. They operate programs and ministries with the aim of bringing people in their doors who will bring resources that will further sustain them.

Research from an ARIS (American Religious Identification Survey) study conducted at the opening of the decade showed a significant shift away from organized religion with an increasing number of Americans defining themselves as "spiritual but not religious." That same study showed that more Americans define themselves as "spiritual but not religious" than the number who are Lutheran, Methodist, or Episcopalian taken as a whole (NowPublic.com: "Statistics Show 33% of Americans Spiritual but Not Religious," www.now public.com/culture/statistics-show-33-americans-spiritual-not-religious#ixzzltXUqb297).

The findings suggest that the organization that is flexible enough to meet people where they are in their "spiritual but not religious" state and enter into faith conversations with them will be much more effective than organizations that keep doing what they have been doing, hoping that outsiders show up.

The Go-To Church

What this ultimately means is that the church general and the church local must stop acting as if we are the center of culture in America. We enjoyed that designation for the first two hundred years of our life in America but no more. We can no longer fling open the doors and expect the crowds to rush in; we are no longer a "come here" organization as is evidenced by the large number of people who will not or no longer "come here."

But what is the alternative? **The Go-To Church.** The answer to fulfilling our call to reach the world is to go to the world. Jesus didn't instruct the disciples to stay in Jerusalem and wait for the world to come to them; he instructed them to go to the world. Though our going will look different than that of those first disciples, the command still stands. The task then becomes to identify what a Go-To Church looks like.

The Go-To Church lives by a different set of questions and rules. The Go-To Church doesn't ask, "What can we do to get people to come here?" Instead they ask, "What needs do people out there have that we need to meet?" The Go-To Church doesn't ask, "What about our members?" The Go-To Church asks, "What about the people who live outside our doors and in our community?" The Go-To Church doesn't ask, "What will make our church grow?" It asks, "What are Jesus' priorities in our community and world?"

The Go-To Church also lives by the rule of relationship. Everything is about relationship, and that means that the Go-To Church goes to the community to build relationships that meet the needs of the poor, marginalized, disinterested, and disconnected. They don't assume that those people will begin a relationship with the church, and they become the church that builds a relationship with them.

Exactly how these questions are answered and this rule is followed is as unique as each of the communities in which local churches exist. One community might answer those questions and live out this rule of relationship in a very different way than another community. For this reason, this book is not about the answers to those questions. Rather, this book is about how to customize ministry in response to the answers to those well-crafted questions in the community where you live.

The Go-To Church is not a program that you buy nor is it a designation you earn by completing a checklist of practices or acquired resources. The Go-To Church is a strategic way of thinking about the heart of the gospel, the heart of your local church, and the unreached and disconnected people who live in the communities around your church. The Go-To Church is a way of customizing the mission and ministry of your church to connect to the specific culture and nuances of the people you would reach. This book will show you how.

Chapter 2

Why
Multisite?

Waking Up

The realization hit me as I was standing in the middle of nearly 3,000 people at our largest "come-level" event of the year—"as large as this group is, it is only a fraction of the unreached population in our region." The Orchard—the church my wife and I founded and lead—has always worked extremely hard to connect to people who do not have a personal relationship with Jesus or a connection to a community of faith. This event was no exception. By design our free Fall Festival in the park doesn't smell, look, or feel like church. No one prays, makes any service-time announcements, or introduces any of our pastors. We play secular music, with free food, games, and fun for everyone because we want our community to know that we are normal people who are motivated by Jesus' love for us to love and serve them.

As I stood there, in what could be evaluated as a largely successful event with over 1,000 guests, I wondered what it would take to reach the other 20,000 people in our town, and the 5,000 unreached in the next town, and the unreached 3,000 in the next. Have you ever wondered that? Interestingly enough, I had some of the answers to my questions in my own congregation. We already had a number of people driving from these outlying communities; all I needed to do was ask them, "How do we reach your friends?" Our interest in and development of a Multisite strategy came in response to their answers.

> **We already had a number of people driving from these outlying communities; all we needed to do was ask them.**

A Noticeably Absent Instruction

Much easier than the work of asking, planning, and executing a strategy to reach the unchurched in our town and the neighboring towns would be to settle in and focus on the people who were already responding. After all, when Jesus sends out the twelve in Matthew, he says, "If any household or town refuses to welcome you or listen to your message, shake its dust from your feet as you leave" (Matthew 10:14).

When Jesus delivers his parting message at the

end of Matthew's Gospel, he gives them responsibility for telling the whole world and does not include this prior escape clause. He just instructs them to go tell the world, teach them, and baptize them. His "move on if they don't receive it" message is noticeably absent, pointing, I believe, to his expectation that the disciples in every generation would be diligent in proclaiming his message to all people everywhere.

When we look at Jesus' charge to the disciples in John chapters 14–17, Jesus repeatedly tells them that they and their message will not be received but that they are to tell the world about him anyway (15:27). Jesus seems to be saying that we cannot determine the response, but we are to proclaim the message anyway. I am confident Jesus would explain that we must proclaim it in a way that the message can be heard, be understood, and receive a response.

It was with these instructions in mind that we began to ask the question, "How do we reach the unchurched thousands in our region?"

Barriers

One of the first things our members who drove from neighboring communities told us was that geography was often a barrier to them bringing a friend to church with them. Mississippi is largely rural, and many people drive to work or shop from as much as fifty miles away. After driving those distances Monday through Saturday, they are far less inclined to make that same trip on Sunday. Even when our attendees could convince their neighbors to visit with them once, the return trip was a much harder sell because of the distance.

Of course, geographical barriers that prevent people from attending church are not new in church growth research. You probably see this reflected in your own church. In addition to real geographical barriers like distance, there are imagined geographical barriers like rivers, interstates, and a community's municipal limits. People from one side of the tracks might not cross over the tracks for goods and services, preferring to stay in their community to connect to these services. When you add that churches are often geographical centerpieces in these communities, then you have to begin to address the challenge of getting people to drive thirty minutes to your church when they won't drive three to the one down the street!

Let me make sure you understand that I am not advocating drawing people from other churches to your church. The particular challenge is to reach unreached people in any community who are not being reached. If they won't drive three minutes to a church near their home, then you must question what you can do about that from thirty minutes away—especially when you already have a witness and presence in that community through your members who live there.

Alternative Expression

When my wife and I came to Tupelo to start a new United Methodist congregation, we didn't do it because there were not any other United Methodist churches in the area. In fact, there were already six other United Methodist churches in our city, not to mention those in neighboring communities. Add to that the number of excellent Baptist, Presbyterian, Pentecostal, Catholic, and non-denominational churches and you might say that our town was thoroughly churched. What you couldn't say is that our town was thoroughly reached. Statistics revealed that about 20,000 people in our town did not have a personal relationship with Jesus or a connection to a community of faith. This number is hopelessly low. If you added church attendance in our town on any given Sunday and counted only those who attend as converted, then the number of unreached people would be closer to 30,000 than 20,000.

When we planted The Orchard, we did so with the conviction that there was a communication gap. We knew that there were plenty of wonderful churches that were communicating the gospel faithfully. Almost all of them, however, were communicating it in a similar way, so those who "spoke that language" responded. But 20,000 people were saying, "we don't understand" or "we don't see how this impacts our lives" or "we don't care." Someone needed to take responsibility for learning their language instead of expecting them to learn ours so that the eternal truth of the gospel might be communicated in a way that they could hear, understand, and respond—even if that response was rejection.

> # Unchurched people don't usually speak the church's language.

With that in mind, The Orchard has always worked very hard at being an "alternative expression of the gospel." What we mean by that is we have an alternative focus—we are focused on the people in our towns who do not currently go to church. We are focused on those who do not even attend our services yet. This means that we ask our people to make some concessions about what they want in a service in order that we might continually tailor our services to those who need to hear the gospel message in a way that is has a greater chance of relating to them.

It also means that we have some alternative strategies—we do a few things and we do them very well. Instead of a packed menu of programs and opportunities to be *at* the church, we ask our people to commit to worship, to grow as disciples, and to impact our community by *being* the church outside our doors. This leads to some alternative practices like casual dress, storefront worship spaces, upbeat music styles, and asking our guests not to feel obligated to give money during the offering time. With all these alternatives in mind, we do not preach an alternative gospel—we know that the only thing that has the capacity to change lives is the timeless truth of God's work in Jesus as proclaimed by the Scriptures. There are no alternatives for the Person of Truth, the Spirit of Truth, and the Word of Truth when it comes to life change!

This alternative expression was desperately needed in our community and was what drew people from the neighboring communities to our church. Many of them had never heard the good news in a way that they could understand and respond to it. Many of them know that if their friends could hear the good news in a way that they could understand and respond to it, then they would too.

The Uniqueness of Communities

One other factor that kept coming up time and time again in our research with our members was the uniqueness of their communities. Tupelo is a regional hub with as many as twenty neighboring municipalities that are smaller in size. The people who live in these outlying areas are intensely proud of their communities, often expressing great pride in their neighborhoods, schools, and way of life. These towns express this pride through community festivals that celebrate their history, through wearing school colors, through local politics and civic involvement, and by sharing life together through these communal connections. Out of these histories grow unique expressions of who the people who live there are and how they act because of that shared history.

I live in the county seat of Tupelo. It is the seat of county and city government and the hub for health care, shopping, industry, and the arts. It is considered by those who live outside of the city limits as "the city" where life is busy, traffic is bothersome, and the pace of life is too fast. By Mississippi standards, it is a large city in North Mississippi, a central employment hub that grows to 160,000 people during the workday and shrinks back toward its official population of 40,000 when the workday is done. Though Tupelo would feel more like a suburb to people who have lived in and around large metropolises, it has the feel of a city with many goods and services that would be characteristic of much larger cities because it is a regional hub that services the needs of a much larger population than actually resides here.

Around Tupelo lie rural communities with small city governments that employ part-time mayors and city staff. Communities like Shannon, Saltillo, Mooreville, and Baldwyn all pride themselves on not being "the city" and celebrate their slower pace of life, smaller schools, and more affordable housing. The people who live in these communities interact with "the city" on a need-to basis. If they don't need to interact with the city, then they don't. They go to school in their communities, go to sporting events at those schools, run for office and vote in those communities, and largely live their nonworking lives in those communities. If they go to church (and that is a big if), then they naturally look to go to church in their communities.

But what if they don't go to church? What if no church in their community speaks their language? What if churches that do speak their language are too far away? What if churches outside their area are full of people whose life is very different from theirs—what they support, what they are interested in, where they come from?

What about those people for whom geography or lack of connection or the uniqueness of their communities keeps them from ever attending a church and hearing the good news that can change their lives and their eternity?

The Answer Is . . .

What if someone were to plant a church near them, one that is aware of and sensitive to the uniqueness of their community? What if that same church worked very hard at speaking their language, interpreting for them in alternative ways the good news of the Gospel so that they can hear and respond and invite others to hear and respond? What if the thing that they most needed was not 30 miles away, but right down the road?

This is the amazing opportunity of Multisite. Multisite lets a church address the specific gaps in proclaiming the gospel in any given community by tailoring the expression specifically to that community. It lets a church address the barriers of geography and, in many cases as I will explain later, demography that keep people from even trying church. It also lets churches and the people who attend address the specific missional needs of the communities in which the sites are located in a way that a centralized community of faith may find more difficult. The heart for Multisite must grow from a conviction that anywhere people are not hearing the gospel in a way that they can hear and respond to, something can and must be done!

As I stood in the middle of that crowd that day at our come-level event, it became clear to me that we can't just keep flinging open the doors and inviting people in. Though we certainly must continue to faithfully do this, we must go to the communities around us asking, "What keeps you from attending, hearing, responding, engaging?" and then addressing those barriers. What we have found is that Multisite is an excellent strategy for beginning to address these barriers and to obey the mandate of Jesus to reach the world as we wrestle with the question of how to do just that.

Why Not . . .

While many alternative strategies address various opportunities to reach the unchurched, Multisite is the most comprehensive answer to most of the questions about how to reach the unreached in our communities. Certainly, planting new churches would be a viable way to address these same needs, but church-planting has issues of its own. I am the Director of Church Planting for The Mississippi Annual Conference of The United Methodist Church and also a church planter myself. I coach church planters and have for over ten years because I believe we need new and growing expressions of the gospel throughout our communities and the world. One of the overwhelming barriers to planting new churches is that there are not enough church planters to plant churches where we need them! I understand that this means we have to be recruiting, training, and deploying called men and women to plant churches, but even then, it is my assertion that we need both the church planting and the Multisite stream of work if we are to reach the unreached in our communities. Let me be clear. I am not advocating Multisite instead of church planting; I am advocating Multisite *and* church planting and have invested my life in both.

A second reality that endorses Multisite is that most churches will never mother a new church. The complications of this reality are varied. Most churches don't plant churches because they think they are creating competition for their church, or they think their church could reach all the unreached in their town, or they don't want to make the financial investment, or they don't want to give away their members to another church or pastor. Multisite maintains a connection to the Mother Church (a healthy one!) that allows for alignment of teaching and passion and for particularization of ministry and mission. While a church plant often is seen as "them," most Multisites are seen as "us," and this distinction increases the support for and the effectivness of Multisites in areas where church plants struggle.

> ## A Multisite strategy will work for all churches.

One final consideration is that a Multisite can be launched in a community where a church plant doesn't make sense fiscally. Church planters rarely plant churches in communities of five thousand people or fewer. The likelihood of a church reaching sustainability for a full-time pastor and any staff in a small community is not very good. In order to approach sustainability, the congregation would have to reach as much as 10 percent of the community's population—quite an accomplishment! However, a community of five thousand and even smaller communities are the perfect place for a Multisite for reasons I will now explain.

People's Passion

The people who are drawn to your church are drawn there for any number of reasons. Maybe they love the preaching, the music, the youth ministry, or the missional focus of your congregation. They moved to town, they visited multiple churches, and they chose yours because of something that made them say, "We want to be a part of this!" If you were to make an appeal to them to leave your church and go be part of a new church plant closer to where they live, then a few of the entrepreneurial or adventuresome types would go, but most would say, "I like it here. I don't know what the new pastor will be like or what the heart of the new church will be like or if I will fit there. So, I'll just stay here."

When I was planting The Orchard, the other United Methodist Churches in town allowed me to make a Sunday morning appeal to their congregations for people to join us in the new work that was being begun across town. I spoke in every one of the six other United Methodist churches in our town, and while they were very supportive, only twelve people decided to leave their church to come help us start a new one. Out of a collective Sunday morning attendance of 1,600, only twelve said "yes." People join your church, make it their home, and do so because there is something about it they love, and people find it hard to leave something they love.

But what if you didn't ask them to leave and instead asked them to be part of an amazing new outreach mission that your church was going to lead. At this new site, many of the things that attracted them to your church will be exactly the same. The teaching will be identical, the music the same or very similar, the children's ministry, the youth ministry, and even the missional heart of this new work will be the same though it will have a community-specific expression. My experience is that people's response is very different.

Now add to that a passion for the community they live in and the neighbors they love who don't go to church. Because Multisites are launched in areas where your church already has a group of people with a heart for the neighbors, the passion for the work is built in. In addition to all the things that they love about your church, they now have a geographically convenient expression of your church to invite their friends too. These same friends will see your church's witness, involvement, compassion, and care for them and the people in their community, and God will use these things to open them to the gospel.

Ultimately, Multisite gives the people who currently attend your church the best of two worlds—remaining a part of the church whose expression and mission they believe in and the best opportunity to connect their neighbors to the good news life of Jesus' community in their community.

> **Multisites give your people
> a way to be a part of their church
> while also connecting with their
> neighbors in a new way.**

New Leadership Opportunities

One of the other benefits of starting a Multisite in a neighboring community is the opportunity it creates for people in that community to lead. Depending on the size of your church, there may be a log jam in leadership positions. You may have leaders who are looking for a place to express their leadership. I know that when we think of leaders who are looking for a way to express their leadership, we can naturally degenerate into thinking about people who are hungry for power. But there are people who have natural leadership abilities who aren't stepping up at your church because they do not see a particular leadership need. Starting a Multisite creates a brand new leadership opportunity for those who, now knowing that you need their gifts, begin to use them. People using their leadership gifts may come from the people who will be part of the site, but in some cases, new leadership also comes when someone who is in leadership at your current location decides he or she wants to be part of the exciting new thing that your church is doing in the community. This creates a leadership void that others who remain behind can step into and apply their gifts to.

We had an exceptional leader and family who lived in one of the towns where we were contemplating launching a site. She and her husband and two boys were part of our Tupelo campus, driving thirty miles each way to church on a Sunday morning. Because of the distance, however, their involvement beyond Sunday morning was a strain and became even more so when both her sons began school and sports and other activities in their community. They attended and were engaged but were not leading—until we had our first community meeting about launching in their community. No family has been more engaged in leadership, more an advocate for mission in that community, or more involved in every aspect of that site than this family who was lying latent at our Tupelo Campus, waiting for the right leadership need.

Multisites give opportunity for new leaders.

Launching a Multisite will increase leadership opportunities at your church, and you will see leaders step up that you did not know were there because they now have an opportunity to lead and a passion for what you are asking them to do.

Prevalence of Gifts

One of the practical reasons to Multisite when compared to planting is that the gifts needed in formal leadership at a site are more common than those needed to start a new church. I do not intend to imply that they are more ordinary, simply that they are more frequently evident.

Church planters, in large part, need entrepreneurial gifts, teaching and preaching gifts, and visionary gifts.

If a church planter can't draw a crowd, engage them, compel them through teaching and preaching, and inspire them to catch a vision of what God has planned for the community they are called to reach, then the plant will have a very short life-span. Even where these gifts are prevalent, statistics indicate that as many as 40 percent of all church plants fail.

Several years ago, I was in an ongoing conversation with a church-planting executive about why some of the church plants under his supervision were failing. He had called me to see if some outside eyes could see something he was missing. The confusing part to both of us was that in several of the plants where he was sure that the gifts and opportunity were perfectly matched, the plants were failing. Several of the plants where he was not sure that gifts and opportunities were matched were thriving! After several lengthy conversations, we came to the conclusion (probably not a new one) that church-planting is the right person with the right gifts in the right place at the right time doing the right things in the right way at the right time and that all of that was impossible for human planning—it had to be Divine.

Multisiting is no less dependent on the Divine. However, the apostolic gifts that are critical for church-planting are less necessary for multisiting than the shepherding, mercy, and missional gifts that are central to Multisite leadership. I will discuss these gifts and roles in a succeeding chapter, but there are clearly more people with shepherding, mercy, and missional gifts in our congregations than there are with apostolic gifts. There is a large pool of people who could pastor a site and who far outnumber the people who could plant a church. This not only opens the door for people who have never considered pastoring to step into those roles, but it also allows us to deploy people with church-planting gifts to plant churches instead of subdue those gifts in a shepherding role.

Let me say again, it may sound like I am advocating multisiting over planting. I am advocating both. We need planters to plant new works, and we need shepherds to shepherd new works so that together we can be faithful to the call of Christ to reach the world.

Better Stewards

Let me add one final practical reason for multisiting—stewardship. In the first year of our first Multisite, we added 200 new people fifty miles away for a cost of $100,000. This price tag included pastor's salary, rent, and equipment. To add those same people to our main campus, if we could have convinced them to drive fifty miles each way, would have cost us 1.5 million dollars in building expansion. This was our most expensive site because it was our first one and our farthest away. Our second site added 200 people at a cost of $65,000, and our third site added eighty-five people for $50,000. Each of these sites is reaching people who we could never reach at a cost much less than we could have accommodated them for at the main site. In addition, those sites have now become self-sustaining and even produce income for ministry in their communities.

While construction costs are upwards of $125 a square foot for new construction (at least in our area), rental spaces and storefront options abound in many of the communities in which Multisites are needed.

Our Northside Site is thirty miles north of the Tupelo Campus. It is located in an old Ford dealership that we rented for $2,400 a month with a lease-purchase option plan that would apply half of our rent over a two-year lease to the purchase price if we decided to buy it. The two-year rent of $57,000 was an inexpensive way to keep our options open while getting a two-year trial to see if the site would thrive. We spent roughly $35,000 retro-fitting the dealership and cleaning it up for use, a one-time cost, and we invested $92,000, excluding staff, in a two-year experiment at reaching the unreached in a community thirty miles away.

Similarly, our Oxford Site is fifty miles west of the Tupelo Campus. We began that site in an arts center that had an auditorium we could rent for $250 a week. As we have grown, we have rented a movie theater and now are in a lease-purchase option in what was last a funeral home. Our first year, we invested $25,000, excluding staff, in an effort to reach the unreached in Oxford. Last year in the funeral home, which we rent for $2,400 a month, we spent a little over $28,000 (which would not be one month's mortgage payment on 1.5 million dollars!).

Our most economic site is our Origins Site, which meets in downtown Tupelo and is aimed at a specific demographic. They meet in a donated dance studio for free. Last year, we reached eighty-five new people for free.

While giving money is not the first issue that we talk about, it certainly is an important question. Sites are more economical in many instances than church plants, and they can be started and become self-sufficient in areas where we would not normally consider planting a new church.

Why?

Why not? With the need for two streams of new work (planting and multisiting) and the passion of our people for their communities and their neighbors, why wouldn't we Multisite? With the leadership opportunities that it provides people who have been sitting in the background waiting to lead and the availability of people who have shepherding, mercy, and missional gifts, why wouldn't we Multisite? With its stewardship advantages in a time in which we most need to be good stewards, why wouldn't we Multisite? With 50 percent of the people in our communities and neighborhoods not having a personal relationship with Jesus or a connection to a community of faith, why wouldn't we Multisite?

You tell me.

Customized Ministry and Outreach

Introduction

I have been blessed to work with church leaders in ten different states and five different denominations, and invariably, someone asks, "Isn't one location trouble enough? Who wants five?!" The basic objection is noted, but it is rooted in a misunderstanding of what Multisite ministry looks like. Often, these misconceptions grow from ministry expressions in some denominational traditions or from a bad experience that the leader had with ministry in multiple locations.

Whenever I have the chance to talk about Multisite with church leaders, one of the first things I have to do is help them redefine what Multisite means. I began explaining "why Multisite," but more clarification is needed about what Multisite *is* and what it *is not*.

What Multisite Is Not

Multisite is not merger. Multisite is not a strategy for bringing several dysfunctional congregations together under one ministry banner. Only on very rare occasions does merger work at all, and it never works under the foundational theories of Multisite. Mergers often attempt to bring two or more groups of people together under one new name and identity while attempting to allow each of the groups to maintain as much of its old identity as possible. Often this experience is like putting a mouse, a cat, and a dog in the same room, calling them a family, and expecting them to get along harmoniously. We all know that is not going to happen. They are different animals and have different values and understandings, and they act like it. Add to this the fact that most mergers happen for financial and not missional reasons and the experience becomes not only territorial and painful but also toxic! Multisite is not bringing several dysfunctional groups together under one ministry banner.

Multisite, in fact, attempts to do just the opposite of merger. It draws people together under one missional banner but then sends them out to express that mission in multiple and individual ways. The reason the groups get together is that the members have a shared heart for the needs of the communities in which they exist, and they work together to address those needs by sharing ideas, resources, and services so that they can most effectively and efficiently meet those needs. Multisite does not seek to draw groups together—it seeks to send out groups from a group that has already formed. They may share services (including financial accounting, record-keeping, and payroll) so they have more time and financial resources to direct at missional work in their communities. While in mergers concessions are made so that each group can maintain its identity within the whole, in Multisite individual missional expression is encouraged because each site is working in a different geographical or cultural community.

> **Multisite does not seek to draw groups together—it seeks to send out groups from a group that has already formed.**

Multisite is not church planting in the traditional sense. When my wife and I were appointed to start a new church in Tupelo, Mississippi, we were part of a denomination that provided instant connection and support from other churches of that denomination. As wonderful as that interest and connection from other churches is, we were still what church planters call "a parachute drop." That means that the denomination flew over the area, pushed us out, our parachutes opened, and we landed in hostile territory. Now, as I said, there were a few friendlies in the area, but in the end, planting a new church was up to us. I had to manage the budget, preach, visit, figure out technology, bring the creative element to worship planning, and do many other routine tasks of church planting. I had the support of others, but planning and execution were up to me.

In Multisite, the support structure for planting a new site is much more developed and, thus, much more engaged than in traditional church planting. I believe strongly in planting new churches; in fact, I am the Director of New Church Planting in my denomination's region. However, churches that could never plant a church can start a site, and leaders who should never plant a church could be wonderful site leaders, as we will see in chapter 7. The advantage of Multisite over planting a new church is a more developed and engaged support system for the new site than often exists for new churches.

> ## The advantage of Multisite over planting a new church is a more developed and engaged support system for the new site than often exists for new churches.

In Multisite, centralized services such as financial, creative, and purchasing free the site leader (site pastor) to do what he or she does best and not be responsible primarily for tasks for which he or she is less talented. Multisite is not church planting in the traditional sense, but it shares, with church planting, the desire to reach unreached people with the gospel by removing some of the barriers to belief.

Multisite is not Parish or Circuit Ministry. In the United Methodist tradition, of which I am a part, we have pastors who may serve as many as five rural congregations as part of a preaching and pastoral circuit. One of the difficult dynamics of circuit ministry is that pastors are spread so thin over five small-membership churches which may all lie within a twenty-mile radius of one another. Instead of pastoring one congregation of 150, pastors often find themselves pastoring five congregations that average thirty people each. This reality in my denomination is what is behind the question I raised at the beginning of this chapter. Multisite, however, is not parish or circuit ministry.

Multisite, like parish or circuit ministry, ties congregations together, but it ties them together around mission, not necessarily around geography. Multisite happens as people from one location want to see unreached people, who live near them in a different location, reached. This desire to learn from one another in order to reach the unreached is the central shared value of a church and its related sites. Also, unlike parish or circuit ministry, the primary teacher or teachers do not deliver the teaching at all of the sites—there are multiple delivery systems to push the message of the gospel out to each site. We will see some options and how each of them works a little later in the chapter. Though on the surface Multisite may appear to be parish or circuit ministry, there are some distinct differences which make it more effective than either of the current expressions we know as parish and circuit ministry.

Multisite is similar enough to some of our old expressions that it raises significant questions for us—most of which are related to our past experiences that lead to misunderstandings about exactly what Multisite is. Sometimes we need to define what Multisite is not so that we can get over these past experiences and see how God can redeem them as we imagine new ways of ministry.

As important as understanding what Multisite is not, it is even more important to understand what it is. I cannot exhaustively define what Multisite is because it is multi-expression. Multisite has some common characteristics, but its expression is as unique as the Mother Church who wants to Multisite and all the communities in which those sites will exist.

Perhaps the best way to paint a picture of what Multisite looks like is to offer you a snapshot of each of our current sites as some expression of what Multisite can be.

Multisite is multi-expression.

What Multisite Can Be

The Mother Church that wants to plant sites does so with an eye toward advancing the kingdom of Christ in every place. This is not a church growth strategy—it is a Kingdom growth strategy. At The Orchard, we have grown to over 1,800 in worship at our weekend services at our Tupelo Campus. All sorts of church leaders often ask me to talk about why what is happening at The Orchard is happening at The Orchard. My answer is more or less specific according to their depth of inquiry, but the theme is always that God loves people—God gave the life of his Son, Jesus, for the world that is full of people. God wants to use, in a mighty way, the Church to get that good news out to the world. God specifically wants to use the local church that wants to be used for God's purposes and God's glory more than their purposes and their glory. In short, God wants to do something that is utterly disproportionate to who we are in the local church so that God will receive glory and God's purpose will be accomplished.

> Multisite is not a church growth strategy—it is a Kingdom growth strategy.

As leaders in the local church, we are often charged with difficult decisions about how to cooperate with

God's Holy Spirit that is leading us in this direction. One guiding question is central for the congregation, its pastor, and its leaders who want to be useful to God in this way: "What is right for the kingdom of Christ?" Because amazing things and amazing growth are happening at The Orchard, I respond to questions about church growth all the time, and I always say that the most important church-growth principle I know is this: "If you will do what is right for the kingdom of Christ, it will always be what is right for your church. But, the inverse of that equation is not true."

The Mother Church that wants to Multisite does so because it wants to expand the kingdom of Christ by bringing the gospel to people everywhere in a language they can understand, while addressing the geographical and cultural barriers that stand in the way of that message being received. This means that if you want to grow the Mother Church location, then you should not Multisite because you are going to ask people who live in specific outlying communities to stop coming to your community and to stay home in theirs as they reach out to their neighbors. Some Mother Church growth may occur because you have more seats available now that some of your regular attenders are at work in the communities in which they live, but this is only a byproduct. The family of God under the care of the Mother Church may grow, but it will grow primarily in the sites. This is celebrated because not only is the family of the Mother Church growing but also, and more important, the family of God is growing as new people are reached. The sites share this same heart and, therefore, are constantly asking the question, "What do we need to do to reach the unreached people in this area?" Their answers become the template for the site that is planted in their particular community.

What follows are some snapshots of what some expressions of this kind of heart look like.

The Extension Site

Our first site was what we now call an Extension Site. By extension, we mean they are too far away from the Mother Church for regular interaction among attenders. Our Orchard Oxford Site is fifty-three miles from our Tupelo Site, and though it has met in an Art Gallery and a movie theater, it now meets in a retrofitted facility that was previously a funeral home. Because Oxford is a significant distance away from the Mother Church, this site is not just in another community, it is in another world. While attenders at our other sites may work together, shop in the same stores, and attend some of the same events, people at our extension site rarely do.

When we were just a few years old, people began to drive from Oxford to Tupelo, but soon that 110-mile round trip grew too long for them and became prohibitive for inviting their unchurched friends to join them. With that situation in mind, we planted a site in Oxford with Pat Ward, who was our Junior High Youth Pastor at Tupelo. Pat had gifts as a communicator and a pastor, and as a result, our extension site had two primary elements of a new church plant from the beginning. Pat had never had such significant responsibility. Pat had relationships in that community because he had family who lived there, but he had very few relationships outside of family in Oxford. If Pat had to tend to all the details of church planting it might have been overwhelming, but we provided centralized services in finances, creativity, printing, and facility location and management. These services freed Pat to do what he was gifted to do.

If you have someone who is gifted to preach, then you might consider beginning an extension site. The strong gift of preaching and communicating is central to beginning a new work, and when we find someone who is capable of excelling in telling the good news, we can provide opportunities for them to do that through planting an extension site. I preach in Oxford only a few times a year, but our other teachers provide support and vacation relief for Pat when it comes to teaching.

One of the challenges of Oxford was making sure that we planted a sustainable site and not one that ebbed and flowed with the student population at the university that is central to that community as a whole. Pat had to focus on reaching families who live in Oxford, not just students who attend the university in Oxford. The Orchard Oxford needed to establish its witness in the community in order to reach the people of the community. There were already great campus student ministries in place, and we didn't want to be another student ministry—we wanted to be a community of faith for all age groups.

Missionally, each site is responsible for the cultural dissection that is necessary for discerning the best avenues for reaching and discipling to people in their towns. Oxford is a culturally rich community with an abundance of writers, singers, and musicians. John Grisham owns a home there and penned his first books at a coffee shop on the Oxford Square. William Faulkner's home is in Oxford, and there is an abundance of live music venues. With that in mind, The Orchard Oxford opened its doors to artists and musicians to display or perform at events The Orchard hosts. Recognizing the central place of the arts in the community was vital to understanding how to reach out to the community.

While our sites have many things in common, youth ministry looks different at every site. In Oxford, the leaders determined a partnership with Young Life was the best way of connecting with teens and introducing them to Jesus while discipling them. So Orchard Oxford opens its doors to Young Life every week and involves its volunteers in youth ministry through Young Life.

The Video Site

The second site we launched was a video site near the Baldwyn Community that is twenty-nine miles away. Meeting in a retrofitted auto dealership, Orchard Northside sits ideally at the junction of three smaller communities—Baldwyn, Saltillo, and Guntown. The combined population within a five-mile radius of our site exceeds three thousand people. Northside is pastored by Jay Stanley, who leads ministry and mission in that community while only preaching four or five times annually. Jay is a gifted communicator but is a much more gifted pastor and encourager. Jay uses his gifts to develop leaders and to disciple people who come to Northside. He also is responsible for the daily organization of ministry and the weekly organization of worship though he doesn't preach. The sermon is delivered by video from the Tupelo Campus.

The decision to launch Northside as a video site came with the recognition that we would be asking people who had a long history with Orchard Tupelo to stay in their community. While the primary incentive to stay in their community was to reach their unreached friends, one of the secondary incentives was that they would continue to receive high-quality teaching they had been receiving while attending Tupelo. Jay was perfectly capable of delivering this; however, he wanted to focus on leading, discipling, and serving in that community, and our decision to deliver teaching by video allowed him to do that.

If you have a leader whose strongest gifts are leading, pastoring, discipling, or serving, then you might consider planting a video site. This setup frees that person to use his or her strongest gifts while teaching is delivered by those whose strongest gift is preaching or teaching.

Outreach for Northside, because it is located between three small towns, involves feeding the local football teams before games, participating in annual Christmas parades, and organizing various kindness projects that serve people in Christ's name. Their engagement in the community is key to their ability to reach the community.

Youth ministry at Northside is a youth small group that meets in a home and attends a large group gathering at the Tupelo Campus once a month. Eventually, we hope to have large group gatherings at Northside.

The Team Teaching Site

Our last *current* (I use this word because I know more are coming!) expression is what we call a Team Teaching Site. This team teaching model is made possible because Origins meets only on Sunday night. Origins is the only one of our sites that does not currently use *The Orchard* in its name. We gave all the other sites the option of naming themselves, and they all chose to include the word *Orchard*. The leader of Origins, Jason McAnally, and I talked about the name and decided that, given his target group, it might be best to not include *Orchard* in his site's name.

Origins was begun primarily as an intentional effort to address a demographic need, not a geographic need as was true in the other plants. There is a culture of people who are unchurched in our town who will never attend the big institutional church on the west side of town, no matter how hard we work at not being the "big institutional church on the west side of town." They don't want big, and they don't want church. With that in mind, we sent Jason to begin a ministry of long-term conversation with them in order to introduce them to Jesus and disciple them as Jesus commands in Matthew 28:19-20.

Origins began meeting in a coffee shop and now meets in a ballroom dance studio and will shortly move to a renovated building that is downtown only four miles away from the Tupelo Campus. While they don't try to hide that they are connected to The Orchard, they don't flaunt it either. One of the ways the connection is obvious is that, while Jason teaches about thirty-five times a year, the rest of our pastors teach the remainder of the time. This team teaching approach lets Jason devote a significant amount of time to the one-on-one conversations and relationship-building that is necessary to reach Origins's target group. Within this group of "outsiders who want to remain outside," there are lots of faith and spirituality questions that Jason has to answer and he must be patient as the people he is trying to reach explore all the answers. Jason is clearly the leader and primary teacher, but the involvement of a team of teachers allows him time for the critical and time-consuming work of developing relationships in his culture.

Missionally, Origins hands out water, snow cones, and sunglasses at summer musical festivals that are downtown. They engage in feeding the hungry at the Salvation Army and even held their Super Bowl party there in order to connect to people who live downtown but nowhere-in-particular downtown.

Origins has a small children's ministry and no youth ministry. This is because the group of people who attend Origins are primarily single, single with children, or married with no children. Children's ministry done well in this context has a profound effect on the child and the parent.

Why Did We Multisite?

It sounds like a lot of churches and a lot of trouble, doesn't it? Sometimes it feels like that—not most times, but sometimes. However, any perspective of trouble fades when I speak with our Tupelo leaders who attend another site. They invariably say, "I don't understand fully what is happening there. But I sure am glad we are doing that!"

I wish I could capture in words the pride and joy that the Tupelo Campus (the Mother Church of our sites) has when they see the ministry that is happening, the people who are being reached, and the baptisms and discipling that are happening at each of our sites.

Quite simply, we decided to Multisite because we wanted to reach more people for Christ and disciple them. The most customizable way, the most efficient way, and the most effective way was Multisite. Imagine how much easier it is to reach distinct people groups when you have distinct tools in your belt. Our leaders saw firsthand, after one site, how effective a tool Multisite could be for reaching and discipling people, and they have never looked back!

Getting Started

Introduction

Why do we need to Multisite? is a common first question among leaders and boards who are presented with the Multisite opportunity. In chapter 3, I answered the theoretical questions and gave some practical reasons for multisiting, but the intent of this chapter is to help you help your leaders move beyond theory to buy-in, in such a way that you all move forward with conviction about Multisite as a viable option for reaching the unreached people in your region.

You may have heard the joke about the father who, in response to his son's question about the birds and the bees, launches into a discourse about the special relationship between and husband and wife and where babies come from—only to be interrupted by his son, whose question was *actually* about birds and bees. The father spent a good bit of time and endured a good deal of discomfort because he was answering questions that his son wasn't asking.

I don't want to spend time answering questions that you may not be asking, but a decade of working with churches of various denominations and backgrounds has taught me there are some common questions and some common misunderstandings about Multisite, and I want to turn my attention to some of those now.

Helping Your People Answer "Why?"

As I said, one of the first questions we face regarding Multisite is "Why?" The leaders who are asking this question are often less concerned with practical aspects of "Why?" and more concerned with the emotional or spiritual aspects of "Why?" A good answer to this opening question makes the follow-up questions and answers go much more smoothly.

I was working with a church in my home state that had asked me to consult with them on beginning a new site. I was meeting with a group of interested people who were passionate about the idea, but they had yet to convince the formal leaders of the church that a new site was a good idea. I began our conversation by asking, "Why do you want to start a site?" Their answers were clear, but they were not good answers. If I had been the board of that church, then I would have turned them down flatly. Ten years have taught me that they had some of the same answers as other groups who wanted to start sites, but they were still giving the wrong answers. We will take a look at some of these common answers a little later in this chapter, but before we do, I want to give you the only right answer for beginning a site—to reach people that no one else is reaching.

The correct answer is: To reach people that no one else is reaching.

If I had been part of that group that was approaching the leaders of a church and asking support and permission to begin a site, then that is the only reason I would give—to reach people no one else is reaching.

There are a lot of by-product benefits, bonuses, if that is what you want to call them, but all of those added benefits are secondary to reaching the unreached people in your region. It is this that must capture the heart of the leaders; it is for this that we are promised the outpouring of the Holy Spirit.

Common Answers

I have heard hundreds of poor reasons to start a site. I can almost anticipate these common but misdirected answers in advance. Every now and then, I am surprised by an answer, but even then, I am not surprised by the motivation behind that answer. If our motivations for starting a site are self- or "me-centered," then the site will fail. God does not promise the power of the Holy Spirit to do our work or to meet our selfish needs. God does promise the power of the Holy Spirit to advance the kingdom of Christ, accomplishing God's purposes to God's glory, and it is in examining any answers in light of this standard that we see clearly if our reasons for starting a site are common or good.

Music tends to be among the most common reasons I hear for starting a site. If we have more than one site, then we can have more than one worship style or more than one worship leader. What is meant ultimately is that I can have my preference in a leader and style and won't have to keep enduring the leader or style at our only site. Multisite is not a cure for worship wars. Starting a site in order for people who already attend your church to have a musical alternative is a bad idea. Start another service and change the music style, but don't start another site with this in mind.

A second common answer for starting a site is convenience. "Traffic makes it difficult to come to church, but if we put a site on our side of town, then we would be more involved." Notice who is the focus of the request—someone who already attends the church. This answer can actually be a good answer, however, if the people who want a site on their side of town have in mind the traffic or other barriers that keep unchurched people from attending your church.

As I mentioned earlier, this convenience factor was a large determination in planting both our Oxford and Northside sites. However, the plea from our people was for their unchurched friends who would not drive the fifty-mile (Oxford) or thirty-mile (Northside) distances to Tupelo. They commonly heard, "I am not driving three minutes to any of the churches that are nearby; what makes you think I will drive thirty minutes to your church?" When our people living in these outlying areas approached us with a request for a site, their reason was, "We don't mind driving thirty miles to church, but we can't get our unchurched friends to drive that far. Will you put something near us so we can bring them?" What leader could say no to that kind of motivation?

Some leaders want to start a site because it creates a leadership spot for them or a spot for someone they want to get rid of. Motivation here sounds like, "If I help start it, I will get to help run it!" This is one of those places where you have to work hard to check the motivations of the people who will become the core and leadership of the new site. If you begin a site with "all-about-me" people, you will soon have a site that is all about them. Often these people see a site as an opportunity to get everything they want that they have never had at the Mother Church. A clear vision for the site pastor and diligent support by the leaders at the Mother Church are essential in keeping the vision clear and the motivations pure. If you start to compromise on this guiding principle, you will compromise the health of the site and the vitality of the vision.

Certainly, sites do create a place for leaders who have not had room to lead at another site. This leadership vacuum is one of the secondary benefits of starting a site. Leaders who have been developing and are ready to lead, but find no opening at the Mother Church, will find it exciting and enjoy tremendous growth as a leader as they actually lead something. Our leadership core grew exponentially when, because we began three sites, new and more leaders were needed, and they stepped up! However, this can never be the primary reason for beginning a site.

One other emerging reason for starting a site that is not a good one: "Multisiting is cool." Pastors especially enjoy (I am confessing my own sins here) being able to say we are "one church in four locations." It says something about the effectiveness of ministry to outsiders. It is cool to ride the early wave of ideas and to start something new. The creative, entrepreneurial leader derives great satisfaction from a new venture, and when the "business" expands and begins "franchising," satisfaction and pride are high. But this can never be the reason for starting a site. Starting something new just for the sake of starting something new never lasts. In fact, if the only people who go the new site are people who vacated your old site or main site, then the satisfaction and pride may decrease substantially at the old site—where the support, permission, and approval exist. Beginning something new for the sake of beginning something new is never a good idea. There must be a clear idea, vision, and mission about why to start a site. It must be clear with the group who is interested in beginning a site and with the leaders and pastor who will support that work.

Good Answers

If I had been part of that group of people who were asking leadership to support a site, I would have had a crystal-clear answer about why we wanted to start a site—to reach people no one else is reaching. However, I would have articulated it much differently. I would have said, "Fifty percent of the people who live outside our doors do not have a personal relationship with Jesus or a connection to a community of faith. We, not they, are the ones responsible for making sure this relationship and this connection have a chance. When we do not care to go the extra mile, when we do not care to work hard to discern what the barriers are that are keeping them from coming to the church and then work to remove those barriers, we are saying that they can all go to hell. I am unwilling to say that, and I know that you, as leaders of our church, are too. So I am asking you to give us permission and support to be missionaries to that community in hopes that we might connect them to Christ and connect them to the community of faith."

I know that speech is pretty blunt, but I have a reputation for being blunt. You don't have to be blunt, but you do have to be clear, crystal clear, about what is at stake. Beginning sites is not about your comfort or discomfort, your likes or dislikes, your conveniences or inconveniences. In fact, I would propose that people and churches that start sites should own that their experience will be one of discomfort, dislike, inconvenience, and sacrifice; so that in going to the unchurched in an area, they will make Christ's purposes for those unreached people a priority.

The only reason to start a site is to reach people no one else is reaching. There are numerous secondary benefits, but there can be only one primary reason— reaching unreached people.

Making this goal clear to your leaders, or as the leaders of a church that is considering Multisite, is of the utmost importance. One of the ways that we did this early on was to post twenty eight-by-ten pictures of representative people in our community on the wall in our office foyer. Each of those twenty faces represents one thousand people in our community who do not have a personal relationship with Christ or a connection to a community of faith. Our focus is on these people, the outsiders, the people who don't even come here yet whom we call 20/20,000. The short paragraph posted on the wall beside these pictures explains this focus:

In the sight world, 20/20 denotes perfect vision. 20/20 vision lets you know that your focus is clear. Each of these twenty faces represents one thousand people in the Tupelo area that do not have a personal relationship with Jesus or a connection to a community of faith. It is The Orchard's unique call to stay focused on these 20,000 people until every single one of them has those relationships. 20/20,000 and these faces are our way of reminding each other that no matter how many people we have reached, the fulfillment of our call is just beginning.

The first thing people see are the faces of people who are not connected. The number 20,000 can be big and impersonal, but twenty faces that each represent a thousand people cannot be ignored. Helping your leaders see these faces in *your* community is the key to the support and proper motivation for beginning a site.

The uniqueness of each site that is aimed at the unchurched in a particular area can increase the effectiveness of outreach in a community. Tailor-made ministry and cultural engagement break down barriers that are ignored or missed by outsiders. When sites effectively engage their communities and the unreached people in their neighborhoods, it is by intent, not by accident.

Being Alternative

People often ask me to describe the worship or ministry style of The Orchard. We have been called contemporary praise and worship; we have even been called a cult (I assure you we are not!). When I describe how we think about worship and ministry, I say we are an "alternative expression of the gospel." We have an alternative focus; we do our very best to stay focused on people who are not at The Orchard, who do not have a personal relationship with Jesus or a connection to any community of faith. We have an alternative strategy; we want to engage people fully in worship, discipleship, and missions. We don't want our people to gather multiple times during the week, so we have very little off-weekend programming. We want them to worship, be intentional about discipleship, and be intentional about giving their life away—which they can't do if they are always at the church. We are always looking to be alternative in our expression of the Gospel in any community. Most communities have plenty of churches that look like, smell like, and act like churches. We want to be the church that nobody expects us to be in such a way that we break down the barriers so that we can express the one thing that is never alternative for us—the good news of Jesus Christ. We never preach an alternative gospel. We take the unchanging gospel and work to communicate it in an alternative way, with an alternative focus, and an alternative strategy, and our various sites help us do that in alternative cultures and communities.

Wouldn't it be odd, with our focus on being an alternative, to make all our sites conform? With an emphasis on the alternative and on the unreached, it only makes sense for each of our sites to have freedom to express the gospel in whatever alternative way would be most effective for reaching the unchurched in their community.

This freedom leads to multiple questions about who, what, why, where, and how. The what, where, and how questions have multiple good answers. The why question only has one good answer, and that good answer is "who."

I once heard Craig Groeshel of LifeChurch.tv say, "To reach people no one else is reaching, we must do things that no one else is doing" (this quotation can also be found in Andy Stanley, *Deep and Wide* [Grand Rapids: Zondervan, 2012], 305). Sites give us the opportunity to do that thing no one else is doing in more places, more specifically, so that we reach people no one else is reaching. This realization, this passion, must capture any group, pastor, or leadership board of a church that would reach the world through Multisite.

Where DO We Begin?

So you are ready to go, but you do not know how to get started. What needs to happen practically for you to get your first site off the ground? Do you look for a location? Do you identify a leader? Whose approval will you need and how much money is it going to take? Though the details may vary from community to community, consider the rest of this chapter a "quick start guide" to multisiting.

Planning

Research tools are helpful instruments when beginning a site. MissionInsite (missioninsite.com) is a wonderful demographic organization with multiple tools to help you understand what is going on in the communities around you. However, you do not need a demographic tool to know that there are unreached and disconnected people who live in your area.

The latest Gallup poll reports that 45 percent of Americans do not have a personal relationship with Christ or a connection to a community of faith; five in any ten; fifty in one hundred; five hundred in any one thousand (see www.gallup.com/poll/1690/religions.aspx). Think about your office, your neighborhood, the people you are shopping at a mall with on any given day, the people in your town or city; almost half of them are missing something that we, as the church, have been charged with making sure they don't miss.

Consider that statistic alongside the widely recognized trend of people who indicate they are more open to spiritual matters than ever before. Polling data from an ARIS study conducted at the opening of the decade showed a significant shift away from organized religion, with an increasing number of Americans designating themselves as "spiritual but not religious" (SBNR). The same study showed that more Americans define themselves as SBNR than the number who are

Lutheran, Methodist, or Episcopalian taken as a whole. (NowPublic.com: "Statistics Show 33% of Americans Spiritual but Not Religious," (http://www.nowpublic. com/culture/statistics-show-33-americans-spiritual-not-religious#ixzz1tXUqb297). The unreached people are there; what you have to do is identify them.

The surest way to do this is to engage your people in inviting their unchurched friends to your new site. Addressing the missional needs of the community in which you plant the new site will be part of your outreach strategy, but none of those strategies will be as effective as your people maintaining relationships with unchurched people and inviting them to your site.

One of the things critical to planning is determining the ministries to establish first. Eventually your site will have a full complement of ministries to reach the unreached in your community. What those ministries look like and the specific needs they address will be as unique as the community in which your site exists. However, there are some basic ministries that should be in place from day one. Worship, teaching/preaching, children's ministry, and discipling ministries are the four core ministries that we establish with our sites. Depending on the demographics of the community, youth ministry usually falls in the second tier of ministries. Missions will also be a core ministry, but this outreach is such a part of the connection strategy that we do not separate it out but assume that every core area will be involved in our outreach and connection strategy.

For example, we might host an Easter egg hunt in the public park in a community as part of our connecting strategy, but we also know that is part of our children's ministry. It calls on a number of volunteers to use their organizational or hospitality gifts in order for us to organize and host the hunt. We ask each of these core areas of ministry to think about how they should be reaching out and connecting others to the site and to Christ. We don't expect a missions team or leader to be trying to do that work alone.

So, what core ministries do you begin with? I suggest you look at your core families and consider that the families or individuals who begin a site will attract people who are relationally similar to themselves—single people will attract single people, people who are married with young children attract people who are married with young children, and so forth.

> **Look at your core families and consider that the families or individuals who begin a site will attract people who are similar.**

At our Origins site, they do not have youth ministry. They are two years old, but the people that they reach are young singles or young single parents. They also reach a few young two-parent families with small children, and with this demographic they focus primarily on children's ministry and adult ministry. The people in our town who have teenagers do not typically choose to go to church at this alternative site. I expect, as Origins ages, they will discover a need for youth ministry, but that need is likely still some years away.

Worship and teaching are essential. Discipling adults is essential. Training and discipling the "others" who come to your site is a determining factor in what ministries you need to consider as core when you begin your site.

Assembling the Resources

When it comes to assembling the resources to begin your site, none is more important than determining the site pastor. The success of a site rises and falls on leadership, and the selection of the site pastor is the key decision when it comes to resources. I discuss the specifics of what you are looking for in a site pastor in chapter seven, but let me reiterate that the success of a site rises and falls on the selection of a site pastor.

Seeds

The people who commit to be the seed families are vitally important to the launching of a new site. You want people who love Christ, love your church, and want to see the people in their community come to Christ and connect to your church's new site. Getting people who live in a community excited about the idea of a site in their community should be as simple as helping them see the advantage they now have when inviting their friends to church. The best way to assemble these seed families is to hold an information gathering in the community where you are going to launch the new site. Invite everyone in your current church who lives in that community or in a community that will be closer to the new site than they are to the mother site. Then begin to cast vision for the people who live next door, around the corner, or across the street from the site. The people you want to seed the site should not have to be talked into attending the site or being seed families. Their passion for their unreached friends, the community, and the site should spill out of their lives without your prompting. Not everyone who eventually attends the site will be this enthusiastic, but the people who seed it should be. Cast a vision for what the site will be like and what its mission will be, and see who gets on board quickly. If you have to recruit passionate people to seed the site, then it may not be time to begin that site. Sites work best when people who live in a community ask for a site as a way of reaching their unchurched friends. The first site may not happen this way, but subsequent sites should happen this way because people witness firsthand the impact that a site has on a community and the unreached people in that community. They want that too.

Staffing

When trying to discern how much money you will need to start your first site you have to begin by asking, "How will we staff it?" If you have a staff person who might be gifted to lead the new site, then it will cost you significantly less than having to hire someone new to lead the site. You also have to ask if this person will be full-time or part-time. We have begun sites with both. Full-time people can devote their full time to the site, to connecting, pastoring, planning, and leading the new area of ministry. Part-time people are usually working in at least one other area.

Our first site was started by a full-time pastor, primarily because our first site was fifty miles away. It was physically impossible for him to be part of the community fifty miles away and serve in any meaningful capacity at our mother site. Our second site was lead on a part-time basis by our discipleship pastor. As that site's needs grew, we shifted his other responsibilities to give him more time in the site and hired a new discipleship pastor. The salary costs were similar between the pastors of the two sites, but one site cost grew incrementally because the site and its needs grew. The other one was a large initial investment. If you plant a site at a distance where the site pastor can serve a meaningful role at the mother site, it is more economical to give part-time responsibility to a staff member for a site. This approach also allows you to see if their gifts and passions are suited for the site. If, over the course of time, the needs of the site grow, then you can increase the hours of the staff person, or you can fill it with someone new—quite possibly someone who has emerged from the leadership opportunity at the new site.

Location Costs

With the disparity in real estate prices across the country, it is impossible to predict how much you will spend on a location. At The Orchard, we pursue rent or rent-to-own agreements over the first two years of our sites. We believe that, after two years, we will know whether the site will make it or not. By renting, we will not get stuck with property we have purchased if a site does not survive.

Finding a site takes a special set of eyes. I have consulted with churches who are considering starting a site, but they have trouble identifying a potential location. When I come into a community, I see all sorts of potential locations for sites to start. Our Origins site meets in a dance studio, our Oxford site meets in a funeral home, and our Northside site meets in a renovated car dealership. There are lots of potential locations for your site to start, but you are basically looking for three things in a location—parking, easy recognition, and adequate materials.

Parking

The best parking is someone else's parking. You can find this when you rent a storefront to start your site. The parking is either already in place or is owned by other merchants or the developer of your site. The cheapest, and, therefore, the best, parking is someone else's parking.

Easy Recognition

Easy recognition is the next thing on the list when it comes to selecting a site. If you have to go into too much detail to tell people where to find your meeting space, they will not find you, or they will give up trying to find you. Make sure that your location is easily recognized. Our Origins site meets at the dance studio next door to Sprint Print downtown. Oxford meets in the old funeral home at the end of Molly Barr Road. Orchard Northside meets in the old Northside Ford dealership. All three of these locations are easily recognized in those communities. Even if people didn't know that a church meets at those locations, then they know those locations and can find the church.

Adequate Materials

A materials list for starting a site is included in the appendix of this book, but it is safe to say that you must start by deciding what your core ministries will be and then make a list of what materials you need to do those ministries with excellence. That is where you begin. You will discover other needs along the way, but skimping on materials is no way to begin a site. We use the same children's curriculum in all our sites, and the same materials are purchased in bulk by the Tupelo site and then shipped out to our sites. The sound, lighting, and video equipment that we use is tailor-made for each venue. You cannot cookie-cutter this equipment and be guaranteed to see and hear well in the various venues. Our standard is simple: people need to be able to hear and see clearly. Do what is necessary to make this priority a reality. If you do a poor job or an economical job of providing these materials, then people will know that you are not serious about ministry with excellence, and you create a barrier that is often hard to overcome. Video equipment doesn't have to be high definition (HD), but it has to be excellent. Standard definition (SD) can provide high-quality video. Of much more importance is size of screen and clear sight lines if you are using image magnification. The key is that materials and equipment have to be customized to the site in the same way the site is customized to the community. You can make a list, but you must be flexible and discerning.

Permission

Who has to say yes in order for you to start your site? It may be your denomination, your elders, or your local governmental officials. It is important early on to get

their buy-in because you do not want to create momentum among your people only to have those in authority
shut down the site before it begins.

In most instances, you will need to secure buy-in at
multiple levels of your leadership even if you only need
one level of approval. In my denomination (The United
Methodist Church), we had to get approval from the
state level and the support of the state leader (bishop).
Though we did not need other approvals after that, we
did need the support and buy-in of other local United
Methodist pastors and even our own church board leaders. For us, buy-in meant a series of meetings in which
I introduced the site pastor to these groups and talked
through our vision and answered their questions about
what starting a site in their community would mean. I
steered the focus of these conversations toward reaching the unreached in those communities. It was difficult for anyone to argue with a mission of reaching
the unreached in any community. I had to assure them
that we were not interested in recruiting their members or reaching people they were already reaching.
However, half of the population of their communities
was unreached, and we, because we had local people
in that area, had a passion for reaching and connecting
these people.

There are different levels of approval that you will
have to receive to start a site, but do not forget that
there are also multiple levels of buy-in from others in

the community and in your church whose support will make ministry easier and more effective when beginning a site.

Conclusion

Peter Senge wrote a companion to his seminal work, *The Fifth Discipline*, called *The Fifth Discipline Fieldbook*, which he introduces this way: "Begin anywhere, go anywhere." Other than selecting a leader first, there really is no order to the tasks of beginning a site. Start with the selection of the leader, but after that, begin anywhere and go anywhere. The work is much more a process than a checklist. The discerning leader will have a sense of what the next step is even though he or she may not know what the step beyond the next step is.

This is the work of starting a site, and it is the common way of the Spirit of God. Get started!

Chapter 5

Up and Running

Introduction

Almost ten years ago, a friend of mine talked me into training for and participating in a Sprint Triathlon. The course was a half-mile swim and a twenty-three–mile bike ride followed by a four-mile run. I signed up for the race never having swum, biked, or run that far separately, much less combined. The hardest part of both the preparation and race was believing that I could and would finish the event. The day came, the triathlon began, and I won! Well, actually, I finished—which for me was a win! Since that time I have participated in a dozen more triathlons with increasing degrees of success. The first one was the hardest because I was not sure I could complete the course—the others have been a matter of *when,* not *if.*

When you begin to consider Multisite ministry, you may have an experience much like my first race. The hardest part will be believing that you can begin a successful site. However, the preparation and work will pay off, and subsequent sites will be much easier than the first. In fact, there will be a day when your site questions will be more "when" than "if" questions, but that day will be after the first site, after you discover the possibilities and how God wants to use sites to expand God's kingdom in your communities.

The Orchard now has four sites and is actively working on two others. The hard work and the lessons learned from the first site have made the others easier (not easy . . . easier!), but the first site was the laboratory for both failed and successful experiments.

The First Site

Our first site was in Oxford, Mississippi, fifty miles away from the main campus or what we now call the Tupelo Campus. Because there were no out-of-the-ordinary churches in Oxford, we had a unique niche in the market; however, that niche did not assure us success.

In August before we hoped to launch the site in January, we sent Pat Ward and his wife, Sarah, to Oxford to begin the initial cultivation. By cultivation, we intended that Pat and Sarah would find a place to live, engage in the community, and forge relationships. Pat and Sarah did just that. They rented a house, began to volunteer in the community, and connected to people who lived in Oxford.

They also began the detail work of finding a place to worship and finding leaders who would help them with the startup work. Their first location was an old electric power station that had been converted to a community theater and art gallery. It sounds really cool, and it was, but it had its problems. There was almost no parking, and they had to make sure to arrive early in order to clean up from the parties that were often hosted at the Power House on Saturday Night. The main difficulty in Oxford, however, was the difficulty that any site will have when it first starts—connecting with the unreached in the community. In most communities, there are already many churches for churched people. When you try to start a site or church that will reach the unchurched people in any community, it takes a little more time and perseverance because there are often unanticipated roadblocks.

One of the roadblocks for Orchard Oxford was that if a person missed the services on Sunday, it was hard to find them the rest of the week. You couldn't locate the pastor or even the place of ministry Monday through Saturday. We had to remedy this right away by renting office space so that they could be found at times other than Sunday at the Power House.

Oxford also set itself up to face a few barriers. One of the ways that Oxford wanted to attract the unreached was to hold services only at night. They reasoned that most of the crowd they wanted to reach was out late partying Saturday night and that it was unreasonable to expect that they would be awake, much less alert, on Sunday morning. So, they thought, let them sleep it off and then get up and come to church. This was not a faulty line of reasoning; they simply discovered that the crowd they wanted to reach simply did not think that way. If (and that was a big IF) they were interested in going to church, then they expected that it would meet on Sunday morning. If they were going to attend church, then it needed to be one that connected with them in a way that made them *want* to get up and come no matter what they were doing the night before. The Orchard began with night services and limped along until it understood when its target audience would attend church if they attended church.

A second barrier that Oxford established for itself was the practice of taking a passive offering. They placed an offering box in the back of the room and reminded people it was there if they wanted to give. This passive way of "give if you want to" had a profound effect on the financial vibrancy of Oxford, and they remained overly dependent at the early stages. They have since become self-sustaining and contribute to both mission and ministry costs, but a significant step in this direction happened because they began to pass offering bags instead of pointing out an offering box in the back. What they wanted to accomplish with the offering box was accomplished with the offering bag being passed with just a simple shift of language. Instead of putting a box in the back and saying to the committed ones, "Give if you want to," we began to pass offering bags and say, "Don't give if you don't want to." This simple change in the offering practices reminded the committed ones to give in order that the undecided visitors could wait until they had made up their mind whether they were in or out.

One other barrier for Oxford that we did not expect was that we underestimated the importance of finding a location and staying there. Over the course of the first three years in Oxford, the community of faith gathered at the Power House, a university chapel, outdoors at a camp, in a blues bar, and in a movie theater. The movie theater was a great location, but it was always on the edge of financial viability. One week, as the setup team was unloading its equipment for the Sunday service, they were told they would not be able to meet there the next Sunday. They returned later in the week to pick up any remaining equipment to find the doors chained. Ultimately, it was only when we rented an out-of-business funeral home and retrofitted it for use that Oxford grew significantly in attendance and ministry.

When I think about why location had such a profound effect on attendance and ministry, I believe that once Oxford found a physical home, they could focus on reaching and relating to others instead of spending so much time wondering where they would meet and who would take down and set up the things they needed for church. I also think it let them establish an identity in the community—"those crazy people meet in a funeral home!" In a town like Oxford, there were many places available for The Orchard to meet, but knowing the right location and living on a budget in a set place were both key connections that had to be made.

The moving around versus locating question is a constant question that sites must face. There are advantages to both. Moving around prevents your people from falling in love with a site or with ministry in a specific site. However, locating does free them from having to spend a lot of time negotiating places to meet and spending energy on setting up and taking down equipment. The leaders of a site must always manage this tension for the good of the community and the community of faith that will gather at a particular site. For Oxford, moving around for a season was good, but there came a time when the best thing for the life of the community was to commit to a location.

The Second Site

You might assume that the second site was pretty much a repeat of the first site—multiple locations, site pastor, moving to the community, and so on. The reason I am including the story of the second site in this chapter is because it has almost nothing in common with the first site. Each circumstance is unique, and it was our second site that taught us this most profoundly.

We began the second site in a community thirty miles away from Tupelo. It is a bedroom community in which the people work, shop, and eat in Tupelo, but it is also a region where there is a lot of pride in the schools and individual communities. We also had about a hundred and fifty people who were driving thirty miles to Tupelo on Sundays for worship but were finding it difficult to connect to other opportunities or engage their unchurched friends in a way that would inspire them to make the thirty-mile drive with them.

With these parameters in mind, we had a meeting in the local elementary school to judge interest in starting a new site. We had done our homework and knew that there was already a significant amount of interest, but we wanted to engage others who lived in that community in the possibility of reaching their unreached friends and connecting them to a site. We sent out invitations to our people who already attended The Orchard in Tupelo, and we made follow-up phone calls. We gathered in a gym where I cast vision for this new site. We introduced the site pastor and told the crowd we were looking for a location. We started our Northside site in a corner of three communities—Saltillo, Guntown, and Baldwyn. None of these towns is very big, and for that reason, there were not a lot of options for places to meet. We also did not really want to locate directly in one of these towns because it would prevent the people in the other communities from attending. We found the perfect corner where all three communities are within four miles of each other. The only problem was that there was only one location that could serve as a possible meeting place—an old Ford automobile dealership whose building was in foreclosure.

The cars had been gone for years and the building, because of neglect, was in disrepair, but it had potential. Over one covered drive-through, it said "Service," and over the other, it said "Northside" (the name of the Ford dealership). What better words could we have put on our building? We thought it was the perfect location, but the bank that held the property in foreclosure did not. They did not want to sell, and they certainly did not want to rent to a church. Churches were unpredictable, in their estimation, and the unpredictability of the last tenant was what got this property in this mess. We got their message loud and clear. They were not interested. With that option off the table, we began to look at other options, but there simply weren't any. They were too far off the beaten path, too small, too large, or too costly. We came back to the car dealership, believing it was the perfect location, but with no interest on the bank's part, all we could do was pray for a change of heart. That is what we did—we prayed for a change of heart. Finally, the bank agreed to lease us the building at an amazing rate, and they also agreed to give us an option at the end of year one of our lease or the end of year two of our lease to apply 50 percent of our lease payments to the purchase price if we bought the building and land. I wish I could tell you we had to haggle or negotiate for months, but we didn't. God opened a door for us in prayer, and the old Northside Ford building became Orchard Northside.

With the excitement of God's move clearly before our leaders, it wasn't hard to convince them to offer their time to renovate the building. There were some things we had to hire professionals to do, like install air conditioning in the shop where the mechanics had worked so it could be used as a worship space, but most of the other cleaning and painting and renovation was done by people who would call Northside their home. This sweat equity buy knit the Northside site together in amazing ways.

With the leader in place and the building in place and launch day just around the corner, everything seemed to be rolling along until the site pastor determined that he might not be the right fit for site ministry. The person we had chosen as the original site pastor is a great man who had led worship teams and preached and taught from the pastor's position. However, there was some hesitancy on his part about launching a video site and some confusion about how to lead when you do not teach regularly. In the end, he decided that he would take another job. To his credit, he and his family have remained in the community and engaged at Orchard Northside. He leads worship from time to time, and he is loved by the people who attend there—even the new site pastor.

The new site pastor, Jay Stanley, had pastored before and was on our Tupelo staff, leading small-group and discipleship ministry. Jay already lived in the Saltillo community and has an amazing gift for inspiring and connecting to people. I asked Jay if he would serve as the site pastor, at least in the interim, and Jay has never looked back. He is clearly one of the most effective pastors we have, and Jay is loved very much by Northside people. His presence for mission and ministry in the community is amazing, and Northside is thriving under his leadership. When we look for site pastors now, we look for people who are energetic initiators who live in and love the communities in which we place them.

Getting People There

After hearing these stories, you might think that there are only stories of what didn't go well and what failed. If I tell you that over four hundred people worship at Oxford on Sunday and almost two hundred worship at Northside, you might think about those stories differently. For all the things that didn't go right, for all the barriers and all the obstacles, there was a determination and a love for the unreached in these communities that drove our people to keep pursuing God's dream for their communities.

In the end, for all the things that did not go right, all of our sites reach people for Christ, raise them up through discipleship to be like Christ, and then send them out into the world to act like Christ. That is ultimately the measure of success that we pursue.

So how did these sites connect with people in the communities? Both did some of the obvious things to connect with others; they gave out drinks at the local town festival, entered floats in the Christmas parade, fed the high school football team and cheerleaders before a home football game, and hosted free fall festivals in their communities' parks. But for all the things that they thought of and that you might think of, there were some really unique ways of connecting to people that both Oxford and Northside employed.

Oxford is a very eclectic, artsy town. It is where the University of Mississippi is located and is full of musicians, writers, and artists of all kinds. I have often said that Oxford has the most educated wait staff in America because people come to school there and never want to leave. So they stay and wait on tables. It is a great town with marvelous places to eat and shop. Taking this culture into account, Orchard Oxford began inviting local artists to do pre-service music each week as a way of getting people connected to their music. If appropriate, they also invited the artist to sing during the service or post-service as a way of continuing to engage them and engage the community. People who knew the artist would show up to listen or support them, and when they did, the people of The Orchard had an opportunity to connect to them in a non-threatening way.

Northside sits on top of a hill overlooking a major four-lane highway. They were trying to think of a way to connect with people when they came up with what is, by far, my favorite connection opportunity. With the help of our operations director, Northside purchased a billboard tarpaulin. You may have seen these because they are becoming more common. Instead of printing roadside billboards, many billboard companies are printing billboard-size tarpaulins and fitting them over the billboards. Northside purchased a used billboard tarp and installed a giant waterslide on the hill in front of their building and invited everyone to come slide. You would not believe how many people showed up to ride the giant slide. Imagine how many kids saw that and begged their parents to take them to slide down that water slide. The Mississippi Highway Department was not thrilled with the idea because of the right of way, but by the time they told us to take it down, we had been sliding on it for a week!

Getting people to your site is no magic trick; it is an intentional act. There are some ideas that are everyone's idea and they work great, but everywhere there is someone who has that one great idea of how to get people to your site. You have to discover that idea. Just make sure when you get them to your site that you remember that *you did not get them to your site to preach at them. You did not get them to your site to corner them about coming to church.* You may not even get them to your site if you elect to have your event off-site. The real reason you get people to your site or the location of your event is to have an opportunity to connect with them. One of the most effective ways to reach people is to relate to them. When you are planning your sites and you are brainstorming about ways to get people to your site, ask yourself if this connection opportunity will give you the chance to be in conversation with people, to relate to people who do not know Jesus or have a connection to a community of faith. The opportunity to be in conversation and to relate to people is a key to reaching people, connecting with people, and sending people. That is the key to getting a site up and running.

The Fully Functioning Site

Introduction

The most difficult relationship is the parent-child relationship. This is true in the family relationships that we enjoy and is no less true of the Mother Church–site church relationship. We also know that the most rewarding relationships often are the most difficult relationships.

By the word *difficult*, I don't mean to suggest that these relationships must be tension-filled, strained, or uncomfortable. I simply mean that the relationship is ever evolving, and the way we related to one another at the beginning of a relationship is not the same way we relate to one another now.

I have a thirteen-year-old daughter. When she was born, she was completely dependent on me for everything—sustenance (food), protection (shelter and clothing), and an emotional support structure in which she could grow and mature. Over her growing-up years, however, she has become more and more independent, and she now provides many things for herself that she couldn't just a short time ago. However, she is still dependent on me for many of the things she is not ready to handle. She bathes and dresses herself. She organizes her schedule. She can do a lot for herself and even help others with needs they have instead of always being the needy one. However, she doesn't have the buying power to purchase a home, a car, or to pay her cell phone bill by herself. There are a number of ways that I am still the provider, and she is dependent on me.

I have enjoyed watching her mature and become more independent, and I expect that trend to continue. One day, she will be able to provide for herself in almost every way. There may be a day where, functionally, she does not need me at all. However, she will always be connected to me relationally. She came from me, grew up under my care, and will be able to express herself and exist individually some day—yet will remain forever my daughter.

With her maturing must come my maturing. If I treat her, at thirteen, like I treated her at thirteen months or even six years old, then there will be rebellion and rightly so. It is the aim of good parenting to raise Christ-centered, healthy, well-adjusted, independent children who have healthy relationships with their family of origin. Anything less is a loss for everyone involved, and so this work is difficult. It is in this sense that I mean the parent-child relationship is difficult—it takes work. It is never settled. It takes constant attention and growth by both parent and child. This is no less true of a parenting church and a "child" site which is birthed out of it.

The Provision of the Parent Church

In much the same way that a parent provides for his or her children, the parent church acts as the one who gives to the child what she cannot procure for herself. Many think this provision simply means money, but a more appropriate word for this provision is *resources*. *Resources* certainly means money, but it is much broader in scope than just money. It may mean people, goods, services, equipment, coaching, cultural interpretation, and any number of other helps that the parent may have at his or her disposal which the child may need.

When we started our Northside Site, we did so in response to approximately thirty people who lived in that geographical area who wanted near them a site to which they could invite their unchurched friends. It only made sense for us to start by giving that site those thirty leaders who had a heart and vision for what a site could be in that community. However, we also had hundreds of other people who attended the Tupelo Campus, some of them driving over fifteen miles to Tupelo. It also made sense for us to give those thirty leaders access to any of those people who wanted to attend the new campus. When the time came to launch the Northside site, we announced from the Tupelo Campus stage and sent letters and e-mails to all our attenders who lived in the area of the Northside Campus and encouraged them to help begin this new work. It wasn't simply giving Northside leaders; we also gave them other ambassadors who lived nearby.

People weren't the only resource. Tupelo provided the salary for the site pastor and worship leader. We provided site selection support so that, after the people who lived in the area helped us choose a site for worship and ministry, Tupelo's director of operations negotiated the rent and entered into the agreement on behalf of Northside.

We provided the technical people to purchase the equipment at Tupelo's expense or to scavenge extra equipment from Tupelo and to install it, maintain it, and train volunteers on how to use it for upcoming worship services and ministry. This equipment purchase and installation was not relegated to just sound, lighting, and video. Nursery equipment, hospitality equipment, and children's ministry technology and curriculum were all purchased, organized, and prepared by Tupelo because we already had those systems in place. We could provide in a way that Northside could not at that stage of their infancy.

If you hear me saying that the parent should do everything for the child in infancy, then you are hearing me correctly. Parents should use the resources they have at their disposal to provide what the child cannot provide for herself. As the child or site grows, they will begin to provide for themselves, but as important, as a second child or site is born, the first-born will take on many of the providing and caring roles for that site. From the older site's experience, they will know what is needed and what is not and how a site goes about discovering the unique needs of the community and implementing ministries to address those needs. This is not only the way they give back; it encourages their maturation as well. The parent church is to be a provider for sites in their infancy and early adolescence.

Protection by the Parent Church

One of the chief responsibilities of a parent is to keep the child from doing stupid things. The parent, supposedly, knows these things are stupid because of either perspective or experience.

In addition to my thirteen-year-old daughter, I have a ten-year-old son. My daughter is obedient and cautious—not really a risk taker. My son is exactly the opposite; by age six, he had five sets of stitches and a broken arm. One day I came home as he was flipping himself out of a swing backwards and upside down at the height of the swing's arc. I told him to stop, but he didn't. He repeated the maneuver several more times before he missed his landing and experienced the pain I had warned him about. As a parent, sometimes you determine if the lesson is worth the price, and you step in when it isn't.

As a parent church, you have to give space for the site to learn some critical lessons while keeping it from making critical mistakes. You have a responsibility to keep a site pastor and site group from making painful errors that can have a significant impact. Your perspective and experience are to be used to keep them from doing stupid things.

Our Origins site has thus far worshipped in a temporary space. They move in and out of that space every week. While this is good for a season (and often for an extended season because it generates buy-in), we have discovered that moving in and out of a facility on a weekly basis begins to wear on people after a couple of years. The energy it requires to take care of basic needs can often be re-routed with great benefit once a transient site finds a permanent home—even if it is a rental. With that in mind, it has always been our intent to settle Origins eventually, and the search for a rental or purchase property has been underway since the beginning. Of course, because it is Origins's first home, they have been diligent in identifying properties as well. On one occasion, they found a vacant hardware store with a large attached warehouse in a retro district in our town. We toured the facility, and though it was a wreck, we thought it had great potential. We do not mind sweat equity projects at all and see them as another opportunity for buy-in.

The potential of the property was evident to everyone, and the Origins community got excited and began to dream about what ministry in that place would look like. They began to talk about building and colors and ministry outreach events, and we thought we had found a perfect place for a future ministry base of operations. However, the parent (Tupelo) knew that with any old building come old building problems that are more than cosmetic. With that in mind, we were negotiating with the owner based on an independent structural inspection that we (the parent) requested. That inspection revealed that the building was not structurally sound, and unless we want to re-enact the story of Samson and the collapsing of the roof on the Philistines, we should stay clear.

Origins was disappointed but completely understood. The parent church, with lessons learned from its perspective and experience, has the responsibility to keep the child from making mistakes that could prove costly.

This protection extends beyond facilities and includes every area of ministry and mission in a community. The key is to protect without micromanaging. There is no doubt that this is difficult, but the parent should help the child see consequences of actions and step in when the lesson learned is at too high a price. When the parent church asks, "What is at stake if this goes badly?" the answer has to be something more significant than the failing of an event. Children and sites have to learn. Sometimes they learn by failing, and sometimes they learn (and teach us) by doing something we never considered possible. I will say more about that in a moment.

The Leadership of the Parent Church

One of the main support structures that the parent church can provide for the site is leadership oversight and leadership development. By leadership oversight, I mean providing property, financial, and personnel management services that allow the leaders of the site to lead and engage in ministry.

If a site does not have to be distracted by logging giving records, paying the bills and rent, and the selection of the site pastor and worship leader, then folks can be solely focused on ministry that reaches out with the love of Christ in their community. All their time and attention can be given to connecting to others for Christ's purposes. Certainly site leaders would be involved in the selection of any substantial staff positions, but the organization of the process, the vetting of resumes, and the setting of salary would all be provided by the parents instead of the child. In addition, because the parents are providing leadership oversight, they can keep a whole-family perspective that allows the sharing of resources and equipment in such a way that costs savings are enjoyed by the whole.

Every fall, we have our annual Fall Festival with free games, food, and fun in the public park as a way of connecting to those who are disconnected. Our Oxford site and our Northside site put on similar events with the same purpose in mind. Because Tupelo has the contacts, we can negotiate a group price for large inflatables that can be sent to each of those sites, and our purchasing power is increased significantly. Centralized payroll, accounting, and maintenance services also allow for cost-cutting measures because of streamlined staff and office space use. In the end, the leadership that is provided by the parent church allows the site to stay focused on the most important reason any site is begun—reaching people in that community who are unreached.

Interaction between local site leaders and parent church leaders also provides for mentoring relationships that lead to fruitful ministry. Connecting ministry leaders in a site to ministry leaders at the parent church helps them to understand the processes and risks of decisions made at the local level. The parent church leader's understanding of the many facets and opportunities of ministry is enriched by the broad exposure to the unique cultures and communities outside the parent church.

Each year during our leadership retreat, we bring all our campuses' staff and leadership together for learning and sharing. We bring in a speaker or pastor who can address some particular need or area of growth that we are exploring. We have had outstanding speakers and leaders who have had a profound impact on our lives together. However, the greatest impact is always connected to the peer learning that happens among our leaders as they share ministry experiences and decisions with one another. Some of the most productive time is spent between sessions or over meals around the tables in conversation. It is in these conversations that our leaders get the chance to hear real stories of life change in our sites, and site leaders get to hear the heart behind the parent who wanted to start the site. Both come away so encouraged about our life together.

One of the other things we do at this annual leadership retreat is that we ask each of our worship leaders to lead the music before one of the sessions. The diversity of musical styles and the diversity of musical gifts that are all a part of the same family inspire a deep appreciation for the differences that bind us together around a common call. This leadership provision comes from the parent. It is a calling of all the children to come home for a weekend reunion that reminds both the child and the parent of how special the relationship is and how grateful each of us is for that relationship.

The Energy of the Site

Lest you think that all the benefits of this parent-child relationship are for the child, let me point out that the child definitely makes significant contributions too. One of the primary contributions of the child to the family is energy. Add a newborn to any family, and parents will report that they are more exhausted and more energized than at any time in their lives. The energy and excitement of new life, new experiences, and new thresholds always interjects life into a family. This is no less true when a parent church gives birth to a site.

Some of the most excited people and the hardest working attend our sites. The adolescent Tupelo site doesn't need as much attention as the five-year-old Oxford site, the three-year-old Northside site, or the two-year-old Origins site. The buzz is always about what new and crazy thing our "kids" have done this week. Because new sites are a primary way to engage new leaders and new people, you have a tidal wave of new energy and new ideas related to them and ministry in their communities.

The parent sees things through new eyes and is inspired to take risks and to have fun in ways that he or she may not have considered in years—all because of the daring risks and the possibility-thinking of the child. The energy of a new life injects the whole system with life and new possibilities.

These new possibilities include connections to people who would not connect to the parent church. In my personal life, I have relationships with people whom I would not normally have relationships with because our children are involved in the same activities. My daughter swims and my son plays baseball, and both of those activities connect me with others who have children with similar commitments.

When we begin a site (give birth to a child), we begin to connect to people that we have not connected to before. Maybe they considered us standoffish or unapproachable. Maybe they thought we had nothing in common or that our social circles did not interconnect. But when we get to spend time together, it is entirely possible that we will get a different impression of each other. When we begin new sites, people who thought that we were "the big church on the west side of town" may find out we are the smaller community of faith in their town too. They may find that we are not, as they thought, self-serving, but instead, we are very mission and outreach oriented. Our sites give us the opportunity to connect to people who may never connect to the parent church and to give them a completely different impression of who we are.

On an entirely practical level, the sites also give the parent church room to grow. At Easter 2012, 25 percent of our attendance of four thousand attended sites other than Tupelo. There is no way we could have seated another thousand people at Tupelo. In addition, there is no way that those people would have connected to us in those distant communities and made the drive from thirty or fifty miles away to attend Tupelo. Because we had local sites, we had over a thousand people hear the good news who would never have heard it if we hadn't "had a child."

An Ever-Changing Relationship

So what does this relationship between parent church and site look like in the long term? Is the aim for a site to be independent? Is the aim for it to be tethered? And, if it is tethered, how?

Like our growing children, growing sites have an ever-changing relationship with the parent. Our relationship with each site is as unique as our relationships with our different children. Each of them requires a different level of structure and discipline; each of them requires a different level of support and explanation; each of them expresses a different level of autonomy or dependence in various areas of need. While it would be nice if there were a set rule or guide for what to do in the relationship, in the end, such rules or guides are counterproductive.

Every year, my wife and I sit down at the end of the school year and try to make educational decisions for both our children based on the unique gifts and needs of our two very different children. We had an idea at their birth that we could settle all of those decisions on the front end of their lives, but life (perspective and experience) has taught us that we have to ask, "What is the right thing for this upcoming year for this particular child?" I think responsible parenting demands a thoughtful, prayerful decision.

I recommend the same regarding the ever-changing nature of parent church and site relationships. Every year our leaders ask, "What is best for that site for the upcoming year? What will make their ministry most fruitful? What will free them up to do what they need to do?" At a certain age, the sites get input and engage in the conversation around those questions. Sites start out tethered to the parent church. Those tethers change, stretch, and could ultimately be removed altogether, but they should not be removed on an arbitrary timeline or out of rebellion or laziness but out of concern for releasing a Christ-centered, healthy, well-adjusted, and independent child/site that has a healthy relationship with the family of origin. This is the responsibility of a parent.

Sibling Rivalry?

Does this dynamic change when you have a second or third site? You might suspect that, like families, our site children begin to quarrel over resources or attention, but our experience is that the opposite is true. Instead of competing, sites can become the greatest teammates in working for the same goal. Sites always begin with the vision of reaching the unreached in their community and connecting them to the community of faith. With this Kingdom vision in mind, each site celebrates the success of the other sites and even contributes to it with ideas, feedback, and lessons that help each site function more effectively.

What happens when there are limited resources and choices have to be made? Everyone feels the pinch. We would never cut one site's budget dramatically in order to fund another. Instead we get everyone in the room and ask where *we* cut back in order that we may all continue to have effective ministry. Certainly some sites cost more than others, and there are cost-intensive times in each site's life (for instance. when they move into their first location or when they hire necessary staff members), but each site knows that when that need arises for them, their needs will also be addressed accordingly. When an older sibling goes to college, the costs demand more of the budget be directed toward her education than to that of the younger sibling who still lives at home and attends junior high. The younger sibling knows, however, that when the time comes for him to go to college the same resources will be directed his way. It is not only the job of the parent to manage this cycle of need within budgeted resources, but it is also the job of the leaders to help the sites see and buy into this family approach to ministry. We are all in this together! Being in this together has some wonderful benefits.

Synergy

Synergy is a difficult thing to generate. Most of the time, it happens or it doesn't. There are different levels of synergy, no doubt, but relationships in which multiple organizations are pulling in the same direction with astounding results are rare. This is especially true in the church world. Try to find churches that can work well together on *one* central mission project or on a community-based service project, and you will not have any trouble finding numerous examples. Try to find churches that work well together on *most* of their mission and ministry objectives, and you will have a difficult time identifying many prime examples at all.

This can be seen clearly in my own denomination, The United Methodist Church (UMC). Because Methodism was a frontier movement, it is still largely a rural denomination in many parts of the country. We certainly have a large number of churches in metropolitan and suburban areas, but the majority of our churches are located in rural communities. In those rural communities, it is common for two, three, and sometimes four churches to share one pastor in a relationship called a pastoral charge. The pastor may preach at each church every Sunday or on a rotating basis. These churches are in geographical proximity to one another, but one thing becomes apparent to a new pastor right away—these churches that are linked together by proximity and

pastor still only work together on a few ministry opportunities, preferring instead to act and decide indepen-
dently because synergistic relationships are difficult
to generate. They happen or they don't, and in most
instances in the church world, they don't.

But synergy can be generated when the organizations (or expressions, if you will) spring from the same
heart. Synergy happens primarily because desire for
extension of ministry creates new energy and passion
that, in turn, produce even more synergy.

This multiplication is evident in The Orchard's
sites. The central campus that dreamed of reaching a
new community birthed a campus whose passion was
to reach that community, and the combined efforts have
proven more fruitful than any one group could be alone.
This story has repeated itself three times to date, and this
shared passion and energy have increased as the multiplication of passion has begun to express itself in the
multiplication of energy in other common areas which I
discuss later in the chapter.

However, this multiplication of energy (synergy) is
not the only multiplication experienced. You will also
experience multiplication of ideas. When one site has
a problem to solve, all the sites get involved, and often
one of the sites has already dealt with that problem and
brings experience to the conversation that makes the
problem a short-term issue. This multiplication of ideas

also shows up in worship planning, missional outreach, and age-level ministries. The "wagon-wheel" doesn't have to be re-created; it just has to be reused in a new location or site.

Finally, this multiplying factor shows up in the multiplication of effort. When one campus is using an idea or outreach that another campus developed or has been using for years, staff and key lay people can lend invaluable insights and on-the-ground details about how to make the particulars of that ministry or mission most effective.

As noted before, synergy is a difficult thing to generate. It happens or it doesn't. There are different levels of synergy, no doubt, but relationships in which multiple organizations are pulling in the same direction with astounding results are rare, but not non-existent. This synergy is one of the key characteristics of multiple-site ministry.

What does this synergy look like practically speaking?

What We Share

Children's Ministry

One of the most synergistic sharings happens around the teaching material in multiple sites. This means that curriculum in every age group is the same; therefore, training, resourcing, and even teacher substitutions become streamlined. For example, if all of your sites are using the same children's curriculum, then one teacher training held at one site can effectively prepare multiple teachers. This combination of resources also gets a boost when the training is moved from site to site. Being in another site's space, teachers can get ideas, encourage one another, and get inspired about what someone else is doing with the same curriculum.

Preaching

This synergy around teaching does not stop with children's curriculum but extends even through the preaching and the preparation to preach. Twice a year, our preachers from across the sites gather to plan the teaching schedule for the next teaching cycle. We used to plan a calendar year at a time, but the rhythm of the teaching year is not ideally situated within the calendar year. For that reason, we plan from the end of the fall launch through Easter and from Easter through the fall launch sermon series. All our preachers and teachers from across our sites come together in one room and prayerfully post sermon series ideas that address the teaching needs and felt needs of our congregations.

We then see how those series fit the preaching calendar and begin to divide up text research, commentary work, and even sermon outline work to be shared with all our preachers. This shared preparation allows for efficiency of preparation, but it also helps me see texts and issues from our other preachers' perspectives. It also forces me to deal with texts and issues that I might avoid. This practice enriches my preaching and leads me to insights I might not ever come to if my preparation were in isolation.

Finally, because we have planned together and prepared together, we can preach together. I can preach one sermon to four different gatherings, and if need be, in a four-part series, each preacher can deliver his or her sermon at each of our four different locations. The synergy and learning this practice creates gives depth, breadth, and texture to our preaching that would be impossible without this common work.

Learning and Ideas

One of the greatest synergistic practices is learning that is shared among our various groups. Our preachers range in age from twenty-six to fifty-three, and so our cultural perspectives, generational experiences, and interests are all very different. When one of the younger guys shares something he is reading with me, it makes my world larger, my understanding more informed, and my decision making different. Whether it is a blog post, a video, or a book that is shared across our group, the impact is broadened by having so many people bringing so many different resources to the group.

One of the practices that makes this even more efficient and useful is that, when we share a resource, we often preface it with a comment about how much time reviewing the resource is worth. For example, I may read a book that is worth reading by everyone on our staff and I tell them. Often I read a book and think, "Here are the pertinent ideas or sections that one of our staff or a particular group of our staff might find helpful," and I recommend that part. Sometimes, I even say, "I read a great book. It is not really worth your time reading it, but here are some highlights." Again, this sharing of learning and ideas broadens my worldview and enriches the knowledge base from which I interact with our people and the world.

This practice of sharing learning and ideas is not just for the preachers or the staff. It happens in all kinds of ministry groupings of people who have shared interests or shared ministry responsibilities. Our children's ministers, stage designers, worship leaders, youth ministers, and administrative assistants all share learning and ideas across the sites. This practice is not limited to staff either.

Every year we have a leadership retreat that involves all our staff across the sites and all our leaders across the sites. We bring in a teacher or leader to invest in the spiritual and leadership lives of our people, but a significant portion of our time over a weekend is devoted to sharing learning. When our leaders get together, they share ideas, dreams, and insights, and the result is amazing! Many of the new ideas that we have worked on at the Tupelo Campus were inspired by ideas from the other campuses. Our leaders develop friendships and synergistic leading relationships that they consult and learn from for years to come.

Leadership Oversight

It is difficult to be unified if you operate sites as different entities with different objectives. The synergy of sites is build around the idea of "one church, many locations." This allows for the diversity of expression we have talked about while uniting these diverse expressions around a common heart. This common heart is best kept by a shared leadership structure. At The Orchard, we have a board that we call the Leadership Team. This Leadership Team is responsible for the property, financial, and personnel oversight of all the sites. This unification of responsibility prevents the Leadership Team from becoming territorial over their site and encourages them to keep the big picture in mind as they are making decisions. They cannot compete for resources; they must steward resources for the whole. Each site obviously has significant input and often directs responsibility for the day-to-day management of property, finances, and staff, but larger-scale oversight belongs to one common Leadership Team.

In addition to the Leadership Team, The Orchard also has a group that functions as biblical elders as outlined in 1 Timothy 3 and Titus 1. This group is responsible for the spiritual direction of all our sites. They are the ones who are primarily, with the Senior Pastor, the keepers of the vision. This brings spiritual maturation, selflessness, and wisdom to the oversight of ministry. They are involved in teaching ministry and are our influencers for Kingdom work. They have this responsibility across all our sites.

In order to lead across all our sites, we expect that all our leaders will visit all our sites, and we ask them to visit four times a year the three sites that are not the place they primarily worship. With twenty-five leaders visiting four times a year, we have one hundred visits outside of a leader's primary worship site. This perspective always unifies our leaders and teaches them something about ministry in other places. My favorite reports from these visits always come after one of our leaders has visited our Origins site. The Origins site reaches people who are unlike most of the people who attend our other sites. Whenever one of our leaders comes back from Origins, I can almost recite what they will say: "I visited Origins last night. It was great! I have no idea what they are doing and I don't fit there, but we absolutely have to keep doing that ministry. We are making a difference there!" That is what I want to hear from our leaders.

There are some ministry site leaders who are specific to each site, but this common leadership oversight is essential to the unity of purpose and vision if you want to have "one church, many locations."

Centralized Services

In addition to some practices and oversight we share, we also have some shared services that, in addition to increasing efficiency, also provide cost savings to the overhead budget and thus free up more resources for ministry.

At The Orchard, we employ a Video Director and audio/visual technical staff who are responsible for video, sound, lights, and projection at all our sites. These staff people have an inventory of equipment across our sites that allows the sharing of equipment and saves money on the purchase or rental of equipment for special occasions.

Record keeping such as membership and financial-giving records are also centralized services. One staff person for the all the sites keeps site-specific, yet all-in-one, membership rolls. When a member is received, or a baptism or funeral is performed, all the membership details are handled by a centralized staff person who keeps the records for all the sites. This same centralized staff records all the giving across the sites and sends out giving statements and tax statements to contributors. This allows the sites to be interdependent financially, and this interdependence fosters independence more quickly at each site than if they were left to stand (or fall) alone.

Last, because all the giving records are kept centrally, so too are all the bills, salaries, and operating expenses handled centrally. This means that pastors at our sites get to be *pastors* at our sites and not administrators of details that keep them from leading and doing what they do best. Rent, overhead, repairs, payroll, and maintenance are handled by a Director of Operations who is responsible for all sites.

For all that we share, however, there are some things that must remain unique. Remember we are not aiming for clones. We are hoping for children who share our DNA but have personalized expressions that are appropriate for the ministry context in which they find themselves.

What Is Unique

Leaders

The uniqueness of our sites begins with their leaders. Site pastors are encouraged to be uniquely themselves. We do not try to conform their personalities or gifts to a certain set. We simply want gifted people who lead in the core emphases that we set for our life together. Addressing these core emphases should be as unique as the communities in which our sites exist, and we encourage that uniqueness. Each of our site pastors has different strengths and weaknesses, and each one leads and adds support staff accordingly.

Worship Leading and Service Design

All our worship leaders have different styles, and it would be unfair to ask them all to sing the same songs every Sunday. We do want to choose songs that are sound biblically and theologically. We don't want to be trendy, but outside of these basic guidelines, we allow our worship leaders and their teams to choose their own worship songs for each service.

Our worship leaders across the sites get together regularly and work together and share ideas and songs, but song choice for the service is the responsibility of the worship leader in conversation with the person who is preaching that day.

This freedom extends to worship planning and the design of the worship service. As I have told you, the communities in which we have sites have many similarities, but they also have significant differences. What might make sense in one community might not make sense at all in another. For this reason, the order and pieces of the worship service are planned by the local team with that community and that faith community in mind.

Sermon Series

Not *every* sermon or sermon series has to come from the common planning time. Our preachers face circumstances every day and circumstances in their unique communities which demand specific address. There is freedom to preach and teach with each specific site's needs in mind. However, this practice is encouraged for specific needs, not casual or lazy reasons. If there is a legitimate reason to preach and teach in a direction related to your specific site, then you are encouraged to do so; if not, then let's work together.

Mission Enactment

This same principle is applied to the missional engagement of each site in its community. We expect that each of our sites will branch out with the love of Jesus to the community in which they live. We don't prescribe how they should do that. We can give them some ideas, we can help them figure it out if they need us to, but we never tell them specifically, "Do this." We expect them to branch out with the love of Jesus, and they have to figure out what that means in their context.

Youth Ministry, Men's Ministry, Women's Ministry

Age-level ministries outside of the common children's ministries are also left up to each site. Our Oxford Site has a men's breakfast one morning a week; Tupelo does seasonal men's and women's ministry; Northside has no specific ministry to men currently. Origins disciples men in groups of three in various meetings and places throughout the week. The point is that there is the diversity of expression across the sites but the singular nature of the focus. Age-level ministry must happen in some way, but each site has to figure out what that way is.

This uniqueness is seen most clearly in youth ministry. At Tupelo, our high school students meet together once a month and then in homes the other three weeks. Our junior high students meet weekly for large-group teaching and then small-group study. At Northside, our students simply meet in home groups. In Oxford, we partner with Young Life, which uses our building for ministry gatherings and lets us be a relational part of reaching students in that area. Cookie-cutter youth ministry will not work. We are finding that it will not work with adults either, and unity of purpose with diversity of expression has to be a central principle of a church with multiple sites.

Local Ministry Teams

While general oversight of all sites is provided by a common team, local ministry decisions are best made by people on the ground where those decisions need to be made. For this reason, each of our sites has a Local Ministry Team (LMT) that helps the pastor lead ministry in that specific community. While the Leadership Team sets the budget for a site, the LMT decides how to spend it. While the Leadership Team would give final approval to a staff hire, the LMT would screen, interview, and recommend the preferred candidate. The Leadership Team would give final approval to any facility rental or lease, but the LMT would discern which facility in what part of town was most conducive to ministry. The LMT also helps make the day-to-day ministry decisions by providing the pastor with a team of people who love and want to reach the people of their community. The Local Ministry Team are the leaders of the site and are primarily responsible for the day-to-day opportunities for ministry that are unique to their community.

Conclusion

Synergy is a difficult thing to generate. Most of the time, it happens or it doesn't; there is not a lot of in-between. But synergy can be generated when the organizations spring from the same heart. This happens primarily because desire for extension of ministry creates an energy and passion whose natural outcome is a new expression born of that energy and passion. From these relationships that hold some things in common while allowing for unique expressions, new Kingdom ventures go farther than they could go alone. This synergy multiplies even more forcefully when it happens within a family.

Growing
Deep and
Branching Out
in Leadership

The Leadership Challenge

The greatest challenge in any ministry venture, whether planting churches or beginning a small group or Sunday school class, is finding the leader. Many ideas never get off the ground for want of a leader, and many ministries falter for the same reason. This, coupled with the problem of sometimes choosing the wrong leader, accounts for the struggle that many churches have with launching new ministries, which causes them to revert into simply managing the ones they have.

I am not suggesting that it takes a special kind of leader to begin a new site; however, I am certain that it takes a specific kind of leader.

Missteps

When we began our first video site, we chose a leader who had been a pastor and teacher. He was also a gifted musician and had spent time on previous church staffs leading worship. He seemed to have all the gifts that we thought we would need as we launched out in this new venture. To his credit, he was perfectly willing to be the test pilot of this new ministry. We confessed on the front end that we didn't know exactly what gifts we would need in the new site, and he confessed he didn't know exactly how things were going to work either. Both of us were willing to take the leap.

All began well, but after a few months, we began to see that we needed gifts that were different than we had anticipated and different from what he had. At the same time, this pastor began to recognize that in order to fulfill his call, he needed to exercise different gifts than we were asking him to use. It was a six-month experiment that did not turn out like we expected, but it was a learning experience for all involved. We made a transition in leadership at that site, and the former site pastor and his family continued to attend and be involved there even though he moved on to a para-church ministry where he could faithfully use his gifts.

This experiment clarified for us the kinds of gifts that we now look for as we begin sites and the kind of leader related to each kind of site. However, there are some general gifts that we look for in the pastors we deploy across all our sites.

General Gifts

It is a misnomer to label any gifts as "general" because they have unique expressions in every individual. But in general (there is that word again!), there are some specific gifts that may not make a ministry successful but are more likely to break a ministry when they are absent.

Many might think that the most important gift is a teaching gift. While that is certainly important in one kind of site, it is not critical in another. For example, if your site receives its primary teaching from a central location or Mother Church, then a teaching gift's importance is minimized. Others might think that a shepherding gift is the most important gift, especially when beginning a site where the teaching will come from another location. Certainly, a shepherding gift is key, but if the leader can't draw a crowd, then there will be no one to shepherd. So what are the gifts you should generally look for in a site pastor?

A successful site pastor takes the initiative.

The primary gift that a site pastor must have is initiative. Because a site pastor can feel like or may actually be an Associate Pastor but have the responsibilities as the only pastor at a site, the site pastor has to be someone who is decisive and who can execute the decisions once they are made. If the site pastor waits around for edicts to be handed down from the Mother Church before acting, then that site will never get anything done. It should be the assumption of the leadership at the Mother Church that the site pastor knows the community, understands the needs, and is making decisions with that community in mind—decisions that could not be made by the Mother Church because they are not currently engaged in that community.

Initiative on the site pastor's part is critical because, while the Mother Church should insist on certain values in its sites, the expression of those values should be unique in the community, and those decisions have to be made by the pastor who is engaged in that community in such a way that he or she can make informed decisions.

At our Northside Campus, it is expected that the site pastor will live out the value of community outreach that is central to all of our campuses. However, the expression of community outreach is unique to their community. Each Christmas, the Christmas parade is an event that gathers 80 to 85 percent of the townspeople. Recognizing this as a prime connection opportunity, the members of Northside put on drink-dispensing backpacks and walk the parade route giving out hot chocolate to parade watchers. In addition, they build and enter a Christmas float in the parade—something that would have little impact in the towns of our other sites. The value of community outreach is central to our lives together, but it is because of the initiative of our site pastor at Northside that this value is expressed in a meaningful and useful way in that town. The leaders at the Mother Church would have never guessed the importance or the impact of that engagement. For this reason, initiative is gift one on our list when we begin searching for a site pastor.

The second gift on our list is relationship skills. Do people like this person? Does he or she know how to interact one on one, in a group, and in a room full of people? It is astounding how many times we start new ministries or works with people who have a particular skill that would be vital to startup but discount the fact that no one likes them. Sometimes the entrepreneurial gift can fall into this category. While the entrepreneurial gift is important in some circumstances, it takes a back seat to the relationship gift. Many people can start something, but to sustain something takes advanced relationship gifts.

How many friends does this person have? Only a few close friends or a few close friends and lots of acquaintances? One of the ways I judge this is to take a ministry candidate to a sporting event or to the most popular restaurant in town and see how he or she meets and greets others. Does he or she walk into the restaurant, grab a booth, and exude, "I don't want to be bothered," or have a hard time sitting down because he or she is saying "hi" to people and talking with them? If people do not like your site pastor, then they will not attend the site. I know this seems glaringly obvious, but you would be surprised how many times this relational gift is overlooked.

A pastor friend of mine calls this the ability to be "flock focused" rather than "lamb focused." This is not to say that individual pastoral care and concern never takes place. But if you have a person who is perpetually locked into giving individual attention, then you may have a pastoral counselor instead of a site pastor.

> ## A successful site pastor is "flock focused" rather than "lamb focused."

One final general gift that we look for is a passion for the community in which they will serve. This general gift is specifically expressed by the way pastors become a part of the community. Are they anxious or excited about moving to that community, about enrolling their children in those schools, about spending their lives there instead of back at the home church? They are quite naturally connected to the home church. As we saw in the previous chapter, there are several central service and support connections for this site and its pastor, but the site pastor belongs to the community in which he or she serves—not the one from which he or she comes.

> ## A successful site pastor has passion for the community.

If this passion is absent, then the people pastors are trying to engage will sense it. The people's detachment will stem from the site pastor's detachment. Their engagement will emanate from the site pastor's engagement. The site pastor is the one who, by virtue of living fully in the community, understands the specific needs of the community and the cultural barriers to meeting those needs. Then, because of his or her passion, the pastor discerns, plans, and addresses those needs, enlisting others' help out of his or her initiative and relationship skills.

Specific Gifts

If these gifts are in place, then you can begin to ask the questions about what kind of specific gifts are needed for the kind of site you are planting. While the specific gifts may be weighted more or less by the Mother Church in choosing a site pastor, it is vitally important that you know what kind of site is needed in the area where you intend to start one. This decision will be based on the most effective way of reaching the unchurched in an area, but it will also be based on what kind of leadership you have available. There is no use in trying to fit a square peg into a round hole. Churches that want to start a site should take one of two approaches. They can determine what kind of site to start by deciding what the most effective way of reaching an unreached area will be and then choosing the leadership accordingly. Or, they can determine what kind of leadership they have available and choose a site type and an area in which to deploy that leadership. Either way can be effective as long as the decision makers understand the importance of the general gifts for all candidates for site pastor and the specific gifts that are needed in each type of site.

In a site where the teaching will be primarily delivered in person and primarily by one person, the gifts of teaching and preaching are essential. While seminaries often do a good job of teaching students how to prepare a sermon, they often do a poor job of preparing them to deliver that same sermon. Don't assume simply because someone has a seminary degree that she can preach or bear the teaching load alone. Often a team approach can lighten this load as well as provide on-the-job coaching that can foster improvement in this area. If you do not have someone who has the primary gift of teaching or preaching, then you cannot plant a stand-alone site.

Preaching and leading are inseparable, and it is better for people who come to a site to receive the teaching from somewhere or someone else than to receive poor teaching. The decision between planting a site and planting a church comes down to the kind of leader you have available. A church planter must be able to communicate the gospel message clearly in an attractive and understandable way. Site pastors who are not the primary teachers do not bear the same burden.

Site pastors of a video site must have strong pastoral gifts. While church planters or pastors of stand-alone sites must know how to preach, site pastors of video sites must know how to care for their people. I am not saying that both gifts are not needed by both pastors. However, the weight of these gifts is dramatically shifted with regard to the responsibility of each type of site. A site pastor of a video site or even a team teaching site may only teach or preach a dozen times a year; therefore, they are freed to become deeply involved pastorally in their people's lives. In addition, because they do not have the tool of teaching and preaching to lead with, they must rely on the pastoral tools of care in order to lead the site. They proportionally do more counseling, more spiritual guidance, and more connecting with their people in the community than a site pastor with teaching responsibility will. Freed from time-consuming message preparation, they simply are more available.

In the end, if the general gifts are in place, you can tailor the gifts of your site pastor to the needs of the community into which you are sending him or her. With the general gifts in place, imagine sending someone with a strong recovery background to an area where recovery ministry is most needed. Imagine sending someone with a strong background in marriage and family therapy or in education to an area where those gifts accentuate the ministry and opens doors that have, until his or her arrival, been closed.

Finding Site Pastors

So where do we find these site pastors? The most exciting characteristic of these gifts is that they may be equally found among the professional clergy and lay people. We can employ professional clergy or lay people as site pastors depending on their gifts and a potential site's needs. This means that any effective person in your church could be an effective site pastor.

I think about my home church, a rural United Methodist Church that my parents began attending the year I was born. Over the forty-five years that my parents have attended Salem United Methodist Church, there have been some excellent preachers and some excellent pastors and a few who were good at both. Admittedly, there were some who were not that gifted at either. Because it is a rural church within a reasonable distance of a seminary, many second-career pastors are sent there as they go back to college or on to seminary while serving as student local pastors. I have watched as the attendance has dwindled over the years as children grow up and move away, and I have watched as community and care become more and more a part of the everyday needs of the church in which I grew up. Pastors who are away at school more often than present in the local community, less gifted clergy, and less clergy in general often make it difficult for my home church to do more than limp along. But what if we could offer them a different model?

There is a man in that church who was a coach and a school teacher in that community for over twenty-five years. He and his wife have been involved in caring for people in that church for four decades. Now retired, the man has the initiative, the people skills, and the love for the community that rotating pastors sometimes lack. What if we could provide teaching through another medium and ask him to pastor in that community and in that community of faith? I think he would be the most effective pastor that congregation has seen in many years. That man is my dad. He is respected and loved by the people there, and he has taught Sunday school for over thirty years in that church. Why wouldn't we ask him to do more?

I know that this scenario is a little different than the one we have been talking about, but it is likely that you have a retired teacher in your church or maybe even one who is not retired who would be an excellent pastor and would love to care for others if they were freed from the responsibility of teaching fifty-two times a year. Why not plant a site with them? Effective men and women can be just as effective as clergy as site pastors; in fact, many of them can be more effective! Who is that person in your church who has initiative, people skills, and passion for the community in which he or she lives? Who has the teaching gift or the strong caring gift that could be aimed at people for God's purposes? That person can be a site pastor.

Site or Plant?

This may seem like an odd place to return to the discussion about whether your church should start a site or plant another church. The reason the conversation reemerges here is that what you begin should be determined by what kind of leader you have.

If you have a leader whose primary gifts include teaching, then she will be extremely frustrated if you ask her to lead a site where she may not teach or preach but a few times each year. Likewise if you ask someone whose primary gifts do not include teaching to plant so that he is responsible for teaching multiple times a year, then you will burn him out.

If you have a leader whose primary gifts are shepherding, acting as a pastor, and developing relationships while taking into account what we noted earlier about the need for an initiator, then you have the makings of site leadership. Gifts for church planting, while similar, are unique in a way that goes beyond the requirements of beginning a site. This is one of the things that makes it easier to start multiple sites instead of multiple plants. The gifts for site leaders are more common.

Education and Training

While, at the moment, there is no curriculum for training site pastors, any number of already-in-place curricula could suffice. Stephen's Ministry Training provides excellent training for lay people in caring ministries. I think, however, what we will discover is that there are many gifted people whose education and experience have already prepared them for this ministry if we can help them see it. I can think of at least half a dozen people in my church who could qualify for a site pastor position based on the criteria I have set out in this chapter. If we stop thinking of clergy in the same way, then we can start thinking of ministers and ministry in new ways.

When we identify who the potential site pastors are in our congregations, we will also begin to design training for them based on their needs. Each one will have different strengths and different areas where growth is needed, but their equipping won't always come through formal training. Seminars, retreats, and conferences will play a role in the preparation of site pastors. But apprenticeships, mentoring, and peer learning will be just as vital.

At The Orchard we have four sites. Two of the sites have primary teachers, one has a team teaching approach, and one is a video teaching venue. One half-day each month we all come together and I ask, "What are you working on that we could help you with?" I never have to prompt the conversation more than that. The issues that are raised and the learning that goes on is mutual and comes from each person's educational and experiential background. We are training one another.

Education and training are important but the kind of education and training are not. Find the people and you can figure out the training.

Caring for Site Pastors

I am including this section as a tribute to our Oxford site pastor, Pat Ward. I make this dedication in repentance for how horrifically we cared for him and his wife when we started Orchard Oxford.

On one occasion our leadership team got the bright idea to worship as a whole group in Oxford, which is fifty miles away, and then hold our monthly leadership team meeting on site. That seemed like a great idea, but in the end, it was a horrible idea. The meeting went smoothly enough, and then one of our leaders asked Pat to tell the group what he could do to support him and his wife better. Pat unloaded! Both barrels, multiple shots, and we deserved every hit. They felt isolated; they felt unsupported; and they felt like we didn't care. By our actions, anyone would have drawn the same conclusion.

One significant contributing factor in our treatment of Pat was that he is highly capable. Pat is great at developing relationships; he is a fantastic communicator and has a passion for unchurched people. Pat had been such an effective staff person in Tupelo as our Minister to Junior High Students and Families that we expected he would be just as effective as a site pastor, and we were right. But the support and connection that he had felt as part of our staff and its daily interactions in Tupelo weren't there fifty miles away in Oxford. We had, by neglect, left Pat alone with great results but painful consequences.

To make matters worse, those consequences were shared by Pat's new wife, Sarah. One of the best decisions when starting a site is to send a couple or family to lead the site. Not only will they individually build relationships with people who are unreached, but they also provide support and encouragement for one another. Ministry can be lonely, and site ministry can be extremely lonely when you are sent to a new community. A partner in ministry shares the vision, hope, and joys of reaching unreached people. However, when a site pastor feels disconnected or unsupported, then the spouse also feels that—often times doubly so. Pastors feel it for their spouses *and* for themselves. Pat was feeling unsupported and disconnected, but he was feeling it even more so for his spouse. Even though we had been a source of provision in many ways, we had let them down in one key way—being there for them.

That clarifying moment that Pat provided for our leaders drove us to make some intentional changes about how we connect to and care for our site pastors. Our leaders learned a very important lesson: no matter how efficient, gifted, or effective people are, they still need support, community, and care. With that lesson learned, we began to structure our lives together in order to stay connected.

The first change we made is that we gave one of our pastors the responsibility of weekly connection and attention toward our site pastors. Asking how services went, how their marriage was, what they needed help on, and where we could support them has lead to a healthier relationship between our sites and Tupelo and between our site pastors and me.

We also asked our leaders to visit each of our sites once each year and to make two visits to one of them. These visits were restricted to sites that they did not primarily attend. With fifteen board members and ten lay leaders (which we call The Jeremiah Council) each visiting four times each year, each site has visiting leaders present almost every Sunday of the year.

In addition, we now hold regularly scheduled site pastor meetings one day every six weeks. We spend the day telling stories about what God is doing in our lives, our families, and our sites. We solve problems together, each one of us helping the others discern the way forward in some circumstances of need, and we eat, laugh, and pray together. This regular connection reminds us of what God is doing in places other than the place we primarily lead.

Finally, we learn together. I am constantly giving our site pastors good books I have read or sharing an audio file with them. We have also begun attending one-day conferences together or inviting someone in for the day to invest in our lives and leadership.

When it comes to spouses, we work hard to make sure they know that we care about them. My wife, Wendy, and I go to their community and take them to dinner regularly. Wendy and I invite them to our house, and our leaders always make contact with the spouse and their family when they make their visits in an effort to say "Thank you for all your hard work." We also make sure they know they are invited to any event, gathering, or continuing education that they want to attend. We are still learning what it takes to support our site pastors' spouses, but we are committed to caring for each site pastor's spouse and family because they are a vital part of God's work in any community to which the pastor is sent.

Taking care of site pastors and their families is intentional work. It won't happen by accident. When they get to be on a team that encourages and cares for them, they will serve long tenures and be effective in leading their sites to impact their communities. But left in isolation, they wither and wear out. It is the responsibility of the leaders of any church to care for its pastors so that life happens and lives are changed.

Not Just One Leader

The primary question of a site is, "Where do I find the leader?" The answer is that a leader is in your current site. God has given us many effective leaders who would make excellent site pastors; we simply have to help them see God's bigger picture. Identifying, training, and supporting site pastors is intentional work that produces Kingdom dividends. However, it takes leaders at all levels to be able to make site ministry work. That is why, as important as the site pastor is for your site, the leaders who support, oversee, and provide resources for a site are just as vital. These leaders make the ministry of the site easier or more difficult, and the training of site pastors must also include leadership training and clearly defined roles for *all* the leaders involved.

Identifying, training, and supporting site pastors is intentional work that produces Kingdom dividends.

It is important that a leadership development culture be central to your church so that you will discover those with site pastor gifts and potential, but that culture is also important so you will identify those who play leadership support roles.

One of the best ways we have used to identify both kinds of leaders is a leadership development strategy we call 10:10. The phrase *10:10* stands for eight potential leaders who meet with the pastor and an elder monthly for ten months. I invite one of our lay leaders to help me lead the group, and we lead them through a curriculum that lets us see how they think and what drives them. This ministry was so effective in helping us identify leaders at every level that we now have four groups led by four of our pastors. This 10:10 group meets for two and a half hours every month and reads a book or listens to audio teaching between sessions. We then build our conversation around that resource for the month. A list of the current curriculum can be found in the appendix.

We tried numerous approaches to developing leaders. Bringing in a leadership development speaker or teacher to address a large group of potential leaders was not effective enough; one-on-one leadership development with the pastor was not fast enough. We needed more leaders more quickly. Involving one of our current elders with one of our pastors and eight other participants gives time for discussion and opportunity for shaping leaders in our congregation. This process helps us identify people who have our DNA as potential site pastors and potential Leadership Team participants who can support, oversee, and provide resources for a site so that it is a productive Kingdom venture.

Which Leader Makes the Decision?

With so many leaders, who makes the decisions? If too many cooks can spoil the stew, then too many leaders involved in the decision can lead to nothing getting done! So which leader makes the decision?

In general day-to-day ministry, decisions are made by the site leaders and the ministry leaders of a local site. As each site begins, most of the decisions are made by the site pastor and launch team under my supervision. This is because my role is to oversee and give guidance to all of the sites and site pastors. I help them solve problems, dream, and plan. Ministry team leaders emerge as a site begins to stand on its own, becoming less and less dependent on Tupelo for its life. These ministry team leaders make decisions about mission, outreach, and ministry in their local site. They decide how the budget will be spent and how they will engage the community around them. The site pastor and ministry team leaders make ministry decisions for their site on a daily basis.

The leadership team is a group of leaders who serve on a rotating basis to oversee the finances, property, and personnel of all the Orchard sites. The leadership team receives the budget requests of the sites and sets an overall budget and a site-specific budget which is then released to the site to spend as they wish. The leadership team works with the ministry team leaders of a site to find a location that works for worship and ministry in their community, but the leadership team negotiates the terms of lease or purchase. The leadership team also works closely with the ministry team leaders of a site to hire staff or to release staff when necessary. The leadership team is responsible for *all* Orchard sites and ministries. They understand the big picture and avoid playing favorites with resources. They understand that each site it unique, has unique gifts and opportunities, and also has unique needs. The leadership team's role is to oversee, support, and provide resources for ministry team leaders so they can make good decisions, plan, meet needs, and reach their communities for Christ. (See the chart at the end of this chapter.)

Which leader makes the decision? It depends on which decision, but the real answer is all of them—it takes a team to get ministry done.

Conclusion

John Maxwell is fond of saying, "It all rises or falls on leadership" (*The 21 Indispensable Qualities of a Leader* [Nashville: Thomas Nelson, 2007], xi). Giving attention to the identification, training, deployment, and support of leaders at every level is essential to a fruitful site ministry. Equipped leaders who are all working together toward a common vision of reaching their communities are a powerful Kingdom force. But where there is a leadership vacuum or leadership is fragmented, nothing gets done. The wise leader gives attention to developing leaders who will develop other leaders.

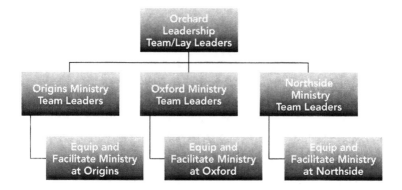

Big Questions

Introduction

By this time, whether you are committed to starting a site or still just exploring the idea, you have some questions you would really like answered. This chapter attempts to answer some of the pertinent questions that did not warrant a whole chapter themselves or find their way into any of the previous chapters. This is an introductory list, but if there are others that you think are vital, please send them to me at bryan@theorchard.net. I would love to answer them and help you launch a site!

What Are the Lines of Authority?

The general rule is that local authority rests with local leaders and the local site pastor. Big-picture authority rests with the leadership team, the ministry board, and the administrative council (whatever you call your board) that makes decisions about oversight, support, and resources.

The site pastors should be accountable to the pastor or overseer of all the sites. At The Orchard, this pastor is me. I talk weekly with our site pastors to review the previous Sunday, including a review of attendance, offerings, and ministry participation. I also meet monthly with each site pastor and focus my time with them around three questions. How is it with your site? How is it with your marriage and family, and how is it with your soul? I also try always to end our time together by asking, "What can I do to help you?"

Additionally, I meet with the site pastors as a group every six to eight weeks for encouragement, problem solving, and storytelling. It helps them to know and experience firsthand that they are not in this ministry alone. While they report to me directly, I want them to know that I am praying and working for their success.

What Counts as Success?

Though measurables are different for every circumstance, our goals are to have a fully functioning ministry of two hundred adults and children that is introducing people to Christ, helping them grow up to be like Christ, and sending them out into the world to act like Christ. Two of our sites are larger than this; two of our sites are smaller than this but growing in that direction. We feel that a community of faith of two hundred has enough community to become knit together and enough momentum, energy, and resources to impact the community significantly.

Financially, we plan for our sites to be self-sustaining no later than year three. There is patience as a site is moving toward that marker, but after year three, if there is still a significant financial gap, we have to consider how much buy-in there is from ministry leaders in that site and the capacity of that site to reach out in mission.

Ultimately success is people introduced to Jesus (conversions); raised up to be like Jesus (discipleship or, as we like to say, growing deep); and sent out in the world to live like Jesus (mission or branching out).

What If We Close a Site?

Start enough sites, and you are bound to have to decide to close one at some juncture. So far we have not had to close a site, but we have delayed opening a couple until we found the right leader. If you have to close a site because it is ineffective or not good stewardship of funds or resources, do the hard work of helping those who attend that site to connect to your other sites or other churches in that community.

What Is the Goal and Focus?

The goal of launching a site is to reach the unreached in a community. Any other goal, any other focus, must be secondary.

What Happens When Leaders Change?

We changed leaders at one of our sites six months in. It was not as difficult as you might assume. The key is to talk to the folks who attend that site. Be completely honest and open, and replace the old leader with a great new leader. Remember it all rises and falls on leadership, and if you replace an effective leader with an ineffective one, then you risk failure.

Leadership transitions are a part of ministry. People discover new gifts and new calls. Spouses get transferred, and leaders in our churches follow with their families. We have been blessed to have long-tenured leadership at our sites, but we know that leadership changes are inevitable. The best remedy for the pain of changing leaders is to have another high-capacity leader ready to take the reins. This is why constant leadership development is so essential.

What Should a Succession Plan Look Like?

Develop leaders constantly, and when a leadership transition takes place, communicate thoroughly and often, use patience, and install a high-capacity leader who oozes your church's mission and vision.

What Does It Cost to Get a Site Up and Running?

Our least expensive site cost $75,000 the first year, and our most expensive one cost $95,000. Real estate costs will dramatically affect the startup costs of your site, but so too will a site pastor's salary, depending on whether the site pastor will be full-time or if one of your current staff will divert some time to leading the site.

Do Site Pastors Have to Be "Pastors"?

No! One of our most effective site pastors is a lay pastor. He has a college degree and has taken a few seminary classes online, but he has no plans to pursue a seminary degree. Some of the most effective site pastors may have very little pastoral or theological training, but you can train them. See chapter 7 on the general and specific gifts to look for in selecting site pastors, and then equip and train them to fulfill this call. Think of how many gifted lay people would be great site pastors!

What Does Launch Day Look Like?

We plan our site launches as soft launches so that we can work out any kinks in children's ministry, worship, or technology for a couple of weeks. We start worshipping in preview services for a month before we go public so we can make sure everything is working as it should.

Launch Day then becomes a focus on any guests that we have and engaging them with our people so that they will return. Launch Day then becomes less stress and more opportunity.

Is Bryan Available to Talk to You and Your Leaders?

Absolutely! I would love to help you or your leaders in any way. E-mail me at bryan@theorchard.net or call me at 662-844-3310, and we can work out the details.

You can also follow me on Twitter @bryandcollier.

Site Pastor Job Description

Purpose Statement: Provide leadership, direction, and shepherding to the congregation that gathers at the designated site/venue under the vision, mission, core values, structure, and authority of the Lead Pastor and Leadership Team.

Responsibilities for All Orchard Staff

- Have Fun! Joy, excitement, and energy spill over into the congregation from the staff. Life and ministry are too short not to enjoy what you are doing!

- Assent to the mission, vision, and core values of The Orchard.

- See this position as a ministry and not a job. We can find many people who want a job. This position is for a servant who wants to help others and serve Christ.

- Assent to a team concept of ministry. We are all on the same team working toward the same goal.

- Be committed to daily times of prayer and Bible study.

- Practice tithing as a spiritual discipline and a commitment to the mission and vision of The Orchard to help others "grow deep" and "branch out."

- Take risks for the furthering of the gospel. Dream, envision, hope, and risk so that God might be glorified, Christ might be exalted, and others may come to know redemption in him.

- Participate in semi-annual evaluation that examines the fulfillment of this job description, being open to redirection and preparation for establishing a vision for the year ahead.

- Attend at least one continuing education event or peer learning event each year at The Orchard's expense. This event should provide opportunities for further development of skills used in your ministry area.

- Work and live within the staff values for community and all guidelines presented in the staff handbook.

- For your own development and the development of others, participate in an Orchard Small Group.

- Participate in the lives of the people of The Orchard through regular attendance at public events.

Responsibilities Specific to the Position

- Be the point of contact for persons wishing to know more about The Orchard, persons needing assistance with personal matters (i.e. counseling or life direction), and persons wanting to become more involved with serving, leading, and giving.

- Work with the Leadership Team in reviewing progress/health of the campus, developing future plans, and developing new and existing leaders.

- Be the champion for "one church in multiple locations" vision while releasing the creative energy of the individual campus (transfer of DNA from original campus to new campus).

- Be available to assist members and visitors with spiritual growth (personal attention or refer to or work with another leader).

- Be the front line for communication and coordination related to immediate needs that arise in the congregation (such as sickness, death, injury, conflict), coordinating with community group leaders and other leaders as needed.

- Work with the Leadership Team to assess health of the congregation and success of the vision.

- Develop relationships with leaders and potential leaders with the intent of equipping them to help people "grow deep" and "branch out."

- Work with the Community Care Pastor, and other campus leaders to develop a means of multiplying leaders who can fill open opportunities.

- Replicate the vision, the core values, and the heart of The Orchard (our DNA) in new leaders.

- Participate in the teaching/preaching ministry of site campus as determined by Lead Pastor of The Orchard's Tupelo Campus.

- Establish a plan to identify and develop prospective leaders for all campus ministry areas (including potential Campus Pastors for other locations).

- Be the weekly worship service host on a consistent basis.

- Identify areas/processes that need improvement, and provide input on ways to accomplish that improvement (i.e. campus ministries, functionality, structure, partnerships).

- Meet with the worship planning team weekly.

Site Worship Leader Job Description

Purpose Statement: Use the Sung word to Prepare us to Engage with the Spoken and Living Word.

Responsibilities for all Orchard Staff

- Have Fun! Joy, excitement, and energy spill over into the congregation from the staff. Life and ministry are too short not to enjoy what you are doing!

- Assent to the mission, vision, and core values of The Orchard.

- See this position as a ministry and not a job. We can find many people who want a job. This position is for a servant who wants to help others and serve Christ.

- Assent to a team concept of ministry. We are all on the same team working toward the same goal.

- Participate in semi-annual evaluation that examines the fulfillment of this job description, being open to redirection and preparation for establishing a vision for the year ahead.

- Work and live within the staff values for community and all guidelines as presented in the staff handbook.

- Attend at least one continuing education event each year at The Orchard's expense. This event should provide opportunities for further development of skills used to lead the congregation as their Worship Leader.

- Be committed to daily times of prayer and Bible study.

- Practice tithing as a spiritual discipline and a commitment to the mission and vision of The Orchard to help others "grow deep" and "branch out."

- Take risks for the furthering of the gospel. Dream, envision, hope, and risk so that God might be glorified, Christ might be exalted, and others may come to know redemption in him.

- For your own development and the development of others, participate in an Orchard Small Group.

- Participate in the lives of the people of The Orchard through regular attendance at public events.

Responsibilities Specific to the Position

- Lead in worship at your site and special events.

- Practice with your team (band/singers) on a weekly basis.

- Work with Worship Arts Minister (as well as Creative Director, Video Director, and Worship Assistant) during worship planning on song sets and specials for each series.

- Worship Leader will follow standard song list as well as plan music specific to his or her site. Work with Worship Arts Minister each month to plan list of songs.

- Work within the process to add and develop new members of the worship team at your site.

- Participate in Worship Leader meetings monthly.

- Assist in planning and implementing the Worship Arts budget as it relates to music, music equipment, and upgrades.

Site Worship Leaders/Site Worship Planning Structure

- Sites will develop their own unique flavor of worship while staying connected to the Orchard DNA.

- Site Worship Leaders will receive a standard list of Orchard songs.

- Site Worship Leaders will select, plan, and prepare a mix of worship songs from the standard list and their own site's list of worship songs. Each month worship sets will be submitted to the Planning Center (under your site or service name). The Worship Arts minister and assistant will oversee the Worship Orders for each site. This oversight is to promote the DNA of worship in Orchard sites and maintain a level of connectivity and quality in our worship.

- Site Worship Leaders need to send audio/mp3 files of their worship songs to the Orchard to be kept on file in the Worship Arts iTunes Archive. This will be our archive of all Orchard worship and a way for sites to share in what other sites are doing in worship.

- Worship Leaders are encouraged to visit the Tupelo Campus to update their own site's iTunes collection from the Worship Arts iTunes archive.

- The Worship Arts Minister will have weekly contact with Site Worship Leaders/Pastors. The Worship Leader team will meet together monthly to promote team attitude, accountability, and growth.

- Creative elements planned for the series including videos, special songs, Orchard Original songs, lighting, and stage set elements will be pushed to the sites.

- The Worship Arts Minister and and staff related to worship will regularly visit sites to provide feedback and evaluation to promote growth and maintain DNA across sites.

Basic Equipment List for Site Startup

These are the actual lists from our Northside Startup to give you some idea of what you might need:

Children's Ministry

- 1 large room for K-2
- 1 large room for 3-5
- 1 large room for large group
- Check-in/ Welcome area

- 1 baby/crawlers room with counters/cabinets and sink
- 1 twos/threes room with counters/cabinets and sink
- 1 fours/fives room with counters/cabinets and sink
- Nursing mother's room?
- Storage area for birth–pre-K/K-5
- Multisite license for Parent Pager
- 2 baby beds (We can provide these from the Tupelo campus.)
- 2 swings
- Riding toy (cars, Little Tike Fish, and so forth)
- Play toys
- 2 bottle warmers
- 2 Lift and Hide toy chests
- Baby play mats/play gyms
- Foam play mats for toddlers
- 3 large colored rugs
- Changing table/mat
- 2 rocking chairs
- Diaper Genie
- Soft play set
- Couch for Nursing Mother's Room

- TV with wired sermon?

- 2 train sets

- 2 kitchen sets with toys

- 2 dollhouses

- 4 horseshoe tables

- 30 chairs

- Bibles

- 3 portable CD players

- Cleaning supplies/paper towels/Kleenex/Germ X/ trash cans

- Diapers/wipes

- Start-up snack supplies (cups, plates, napkins, Ziploc bags, juice, and so forth)

- Miscellaneous environment décor/signage

- 2 iPods

- Basic audio set up—board, speakers, monitor, hand-held microphone

- Wireless microphone for teaching

- 2 lighting trees

- Laptop for media

- 3 DVD players—1 for each room (K-2, 3-5), one for large group environment

- 2 flat-screen TVs to be mounted in each room—K-2, 3-5
- 2 TV carts
- Projector and screen for combined large group worship space
- Hallway sound capabilities
- 6 round rugs
- 4 cube storage units with wheels/baskets
- 4 rectangular tables
- 4 large metal trash cans
- 6 rolling dry-erase boards with easels
- Portable or built staging unit for large group space
- 6 small containers for small-group supplies
- Basic crafts/school supplies/office supplies needed each week
- 2 first-aid kits
- Set of hands-on Bibles—hardback
- Check-in center (will need to be built/quoted)
- 2 check-in kiosks (need to be built/quoted)
- At least 3 check-in computers
- 3 touch-screen monitors
- 3 fingerprint scanners
- 3 cameras

- 3 Dymo Labelwriter Turbo
- Telephones in K-5 area and birth–pre-K area
- Startup administration (volunteer nametags, and so forth)

Sound and Lighting for Worship Space

- Mixer
- Monitor mixer
- Rack
- Mixer lights
- Power distributor x 2
- House speakers x 2
- Subs
- Snake 24 x 8 100 Ft
- Sub snake
- Microphone stands
- Microphones
- Microphone cables (25 ft x 14)
- PA cables (50 ft x 4)
- Direct boxes x 6
- Remote off/on
- Equalizer stereo
- Wireless in-ears

- Westone UM2 in-ears
- In-ears x 6
- In-ear boxes x 6
- In-ear adaptors XLRF-TRS x 6
- In-ear extensions x 6
- Extension Cords (12 ga.) x 5
- Power strips x 2
- Hardware
- TRS-TRS cables x 8
- Keyboard
- Stand
- Cable
- Guitar processor
- Bass guitar
- Percussion setup
- Cymbals

Curriculum List and Plan for
10:10 Leadership Development Group

Month	Resource	Lesson Focus
January	Send out invitations and make follow-up phone calls.	
February	*Spiritual Leadership* by Oswald Sanders	Understand God's call to spiritual leadership.
March	*The Tension Is Good* Audio Teaching by Andy Stanley	Understand what forces and desires drive you.
April	*Axiom* by Bill Hybels	Understand the convictions from which you lead.
May	*It All Goes Back in the Box* Audio Teaching by John Ortberg	Understand what a life of perspective looks like.
June	*Shakelton's Way* by Margaret Morrell	Understand the requirements of leadership.
July	Steve Seamands's 2010 Leadership Retreat Teaching at The Orchard	Understand the costs of leadership.
August	*The Contrarian's Guide to Leadership* by Stephen Sample	Understand how leaders think differently.

September	*An Ounce of Prevention* Audio Teaching by Andy Stanley	Understanding that leaders lead with their resources.
October	*Being God's Man in Leading a Family* by Stephen Arterburn or *Every Man's Marriage* by Stephen Arterburn or *Every Woman's Marriage* by Shannon Ethridge	Understanding leading your family.
November	*The Power of Apprenticing* Audio Teaching by Andy Stanley	Lessons learned and next steps . . . investing in others
December	Year-end gathering at Bryan's house for food and football; nominate next year's participants	

CPSIA information can be obtained at www.ICGtesting.com
Printed in the USA
LVOW122313210513

334681LV00003B/8/P